SHAKESPEARE STUDIES
JULIUS CÆSAR

JULIUS CÆSAR

SHAKESPEARE STUDIES

JULIUS CAESAR

by

BLANCHE COLES

AMS PRESS
NEW YORK

Library of Congress Catalogue Card Number: 72-86174

AMS PRESS, INC.
New York, N.Y. 10003

I heard a thousand blended notes,
While in a grove I sate reclined,
In that sweet mood when pleasant thoughts
Bring sad thoughts to the mind.

To her fair works did Nature link
The human soul that through me ran;
And much it grieved my heart to think
What man has made of man.

Through primrose tufts, in that green bower,
The periwinkle trailed its wreaths;
And 'tis my faith that every flower
Enjoys the air it breathes.

The birds around me hopped and played,
Their thoughts I can not measure:—
But the least motion which they made
It seemed a thrill of pleasure.

The budding twigs spread out their fan,
To catch the breezy air;
And I must think, do all I can,
That there was pleasure there.

If this belief from heaven be sent,
If such be Nature's holy plan,
Have I not reason to lament
What man has made of man?

—Wordsworth: *Lines Written in Early Spring*

PREFACE

In no other play of Shakespeare is the historical background so essential as in *Julius Cæsar*. "Immortal Cæsar," the man who came to bestride the world so like a Colossus that it seemed to observers for the moment to be a "narrow world," must be seen against the setting of his own "majestic world" or the figure loses its proportions and much of its significance. Naturally, Shakespeare could only suggest this background in a play; and, unless the student is a well-trained historian whose habitual thought can travel with ease from one age to another and find the setting of that age, he will, almost invariably, place the characters of another age in his own time and measure them more or less by his own standards. Many students, even with a fairly comprehensive knowledge of world history, find difficulty in untangling from a mass of events the particular issues that bear upon a certain subject. (And, when one who attempts to give instruction in the study of Shakespeare indulges in any such comment, he does it with a smile, knowing that Shakespeare himself was not always particular about keeping the background of the age he was depicting.)

In the study of this play, it is necessary to visualize

the Mediterranean world which we call the "ancient world", but which was, in another sense, a very young world, a world in which there had been as yet no Roman Emperor, no Christian religion, no Christian Church, no Holy Roman Empire, no feudal history, no European nations, no Renaissance, no Reformation, no British Empire, no extent of Atlantic Ocean, no boundless Pacific and no Western Hemisphere. The only way for the average student to get an adequate conception of such a world and to feel the pulse of its life is to build that world from the beginning. To that end I have essayed a brief review of such world events as will throw light upon the period of Cæsar, and have incorporated it in the body of my text.

In reviewing the life of the historical Cæsar, a departure has been made from ordinary teaching procedure. Usually a teacher of Shakespeare must dwell quite insistently on the fact that the dramatist diverges from history and presents his own conception of historical characters. He must constantly warn the student against the danger of confusing Shakespeare's characters with those of the historian. The danger of such confusion is then present in this *Study*; but, for reasons that will appear later, it has seemed expedient to run that risk and to make use of the historical Cæsar that must have been back of Shakespeare's conception, with the hope of reaching a better understanding of the Shakespearean character. The other characters of the play must be studied as Shakespeare presented them, regardless of any historical account.

The text of the play has been treated much as was done in my previous *Studies,* with the exception that the unfolding of the drama has not been followed as closely as before. One may assume that the story of *Julius Cæsar* is already familiar to the student who is ready for this study, and it is not necessary to keep the suspense. As in the case of my *Studies* of *Hamlet* and *Macbeth,* this commentary is intended to be read only with the text of the play.

The approach is again from the angle of character study. "It is of no importance that Shakespeare lived three hundred years ago. To him no psychological problem seems unknown, and he solves them all as if in play. He leads us with equally firm hand to the highest summits and the deepest abysses of the soul. In an age when men had hardly yet put the question Why? to the physical world around them, he had both put and answered it in the domain of the mind, in the human being's own soul." [1]

B. C.

[1] August Goll in *Criminal Types in Shakespeare.*

TABLE OF CONTENTS

SHAKESPEARE STUDIES
JULIUS CÆSAR

HISTORICAL BACKGROUND
OF THE PLAY

ACT I—SCENE I

THE play begins with a Roman holiday. But back
of the celebration of most holidays runs a long story,
often a story of upward and onward endeavor. An
early American writer [1] once said that if a narrator
were to go back to the very beginning of any story he
would have to start with the Creation. Others would
begin with the amœba. The story of Julius Cæsar
properly begins with the creation of the second great
world empire. Previous to Rome only Persia had
ruled over a world empire.

Before the beginning of recorded history, Egypt
had built her monstrous temples, her pyramids, and
her colossi, actuated, we are told, by fear, a haunting
fear of material annihilation. And, as some believe,
she set her great sphinx to watch for the rising sun, in
terrifying fear that without some such material watchman the sun might not rise and the day might never
return. Perhaps it was out of these very apprehen-
sions that there grew gradually a belief in the immor-

[1] Harriet Beecher Stowe.

tality of the soul, a faith that was always connected with the preservation of the body. Meanwhile, having to some extent allayed her fears, Egypt occupied herself with building a civilization—even became for a time the center of Mediterranean civilization. All the world came to trade in the markets of the Nile delta, and the Egyptian navy was supreme in the Mediterranean. But Egypt's day of conquest and aggression passed with the kaleidoscopic movements of the peoples about her, for the ancient world was a swirling mass of restless, invading, incursive peoples. Egypt held the first place in culture and civilization until the sixth century B.C., when that leadership passed to Greece.

Greece, too, may be said to have begun her history in fear, but not the abject fear of the Egyptians. As some one has put it, the founders of Greek society were the gods. The early and popular Greek gods were personifications of the powers of nature: fire, thunder, water, etc., those seemingly hostile, treacherous forces that held primitive man in awe and terror. After a long period of haunting dread, the early Grecians decided that these forces, that seemed alternately angry and kindly, were like themselves, and began to invest them with human and divine attributes and to worship them as gods. Sun, Earth, and Rivers were the powers that they invoked as time went on and awe replaced terror. They gave the gods a home on Mt. Olympus. Out of their imaginative, childlike minds spirits akin to the gods,

Dryads, Oreads, Naiads, came to dwell in their land until every brush-covered hill and fern-lined dale became their dwelling-place, where at any moment piping Pan might appear with his flute and his smiling train. Thus interpreted, the Greek world became more and more attractive and the soul of the thoughtful Greek expanded until beauty became synonymous with goodness. So, with their fears allayed and their everyday world made charming, they went about their daily tasks—tasks that were the beginnings of a civilization. They built their cities, and the sea called to them. They built colonies over the seas— in Asia Minor, along the coasts of the Black and Ægean Seas and in the islands of the Mediterranean. They conquered Troy and razed the towers of Illium; and though no one would dare, or even wish, to cast a doubt upon the Homeric story, the historian is forced to recognize deeper interests underlying the conflict than those given by the poet. "The fact that Agamemnon was able to rally all Greece to engage in his expedition and that the auxiliaries came from many quarters to Priam's help might suggest that more was involved than the recovery of a woman. It is probable that for the Archæan princes the hope of plundering the city renowned for its wealth and looting the cities of subject lands were the direct incentive."[2] And seeking further details of these underlying interests, we find that Troy had accumulated wealth by exacting heavy tolls from ships blown by

[2] *The Cambridge Ancient History,* Vol. II.

storms upon her soil, and eventually came to control
the exchange of merchandise that passed through
the Ægean from Egypt and from the north. So we
find the famous love story of an heroic age entangled
with the kaleidoscopic movements of peoples who,
with their warring and trading, were writing the first
chapters of world history.

Amid all the building up and tearing down that
was going on about her and amid her own aggressive
conquests, Greece built her superior culture; and,
through the miracle of Greek genius, left the world a
heritage of literature, philosophy, and art unparalleled in time. Her greatest contribution to the future
of Europe is connected with her contacts with
Persia.

But always the student of Shakespeare must turn
from the pages of history back to the writings of the
poets; and, before leaving Greece and Troy, we must
recall the story of Æneas and his son Ascanius, or
Julius, whose ambition it was to preserve the Trojan
race, and the prophecy that Cæsar should rise from
the Julian stock—a Cæsar whose fame the skies alone
should bound.

In the mind of the average reader the Hittites were
only local enemies of the Israelites, but at one time
they occupied and ruled over, or had under their
sphere of influence, all the intercontinental bridge
between Asia and Europe. This was the territory between the Euphrates and the Ægean, including Asia
Minor. Asia Minor is to be remembered by the fact

that it became the first great mixing-bowl of races.[3] Records of Hittite beginnings tell of their gods, particularly the god of vegetation, who became angry and disappeared and appeared again bringing new fruitfulness to the land. Some of their myths came from Babylonia, as did much of their material civilization, for their Babylonian teachers had been established in Asia much earlier than they.

Babylonia had lifted herself out of the marshy, reedy sadness of her surroundings to take her place among the peoples of that early time. For, "Babylon is a land not of laughter but of gloom and serious meditation: every evil demon which can attack man lives there, the sun scorches and kills, the frost bites, the thunderstorms are terrible in their assault, and flies, mosquitoes and scorpions add to the trials of man." [4] Into this depressing atmosphere came many local gods, and they mingled in the daily lives of the people, consoling and encouraging them. Local dynasties grew up, flourished and passed. Writing, litigation, and commerce developed, and the donkey caravans of the Babylonian merchants crossed the Syrian Desert into many lands. The great city of Babylon rose behind its towering walls and the great king Nebuchadnezzar came upon the scene, living in lavish magnificence and splendor. The gods remained largely local gods, while the temples erected in their honor became great storehouses of earthly

---

[3] Also we are told that all the hooked noses in the world came from Asia Minor. This would include the Roman nose.

[4] *The Cambridge Ancient History.*

riches. But as men travelled about they exchanged ideas and found new ways of thinking. Their local gods became smaller in their eyes as their minds were broadened by new viewpoints and the concept of one supreme God began to find its way hazily into the minds of men.

Assyria built an empire, but not one of world extent, though it was one of the most remarkable empires of antiquity. It was wholly military in character and was held together, for the comparatively short period of 200 years, by constant war and terrible cruelty. The very name of Assyria struck terror to the peoples who lay in the path of its conquering, pillaging armies. The subjugated territories were held by force alone and, strange to say, the historian attributes the cruelty of these masters to their religious beliefs. The *Cambridge Ancient History* says, "The Assyrians would seem to have been more gloomy and fanatical in their religious beliefs than the Babylonians, and their consequent fierceness and cruelty proved invaluable in enabling them to gain and keep possession of lands which have throughout all history been reduced to order by means of violence only." The power of the kings was limitless, affected only by the pronouncements of the oracles, a power that continued to guide and check the actions of superstitious rulers long after less fear-ridden ages had dawned upon the world. In the end Assyria fell before a coalition of powers which had been trained in siege-warfare by her own kings. "No other land seems to have been sacked and pillaged so completely as was Assyria; no other people, unless it be Israel, was ever so completely enslaved." [5] Ninevah, perhaps the most gorgeous of the ancient capitals, disappeared from the face of the earth.

Persia came upon the scene and played a part that was brave and noble as well as spectacular. In attempting to account for Persia's rise to power, historians attribute her greatness to certain towering individuals, the conquerors, Cyrus, Cambyses, Darius, and Xerxes, and the religious teacher Zoroaster. "Zoroaster conceived of the universe as a great battle between Good and Evil, between Light and Darkness. Man stood in the center of the fight and must aid one side or the other. . . . Such a religion tended not to take man out of the world into a land of meditation, but to keep him in the forefront of doing. . . . It set a high moral standard; it marked a long step toward the worship of one god. It was a perfect expression of national character and it undoubtedly did much to unite the Persian people and inspire them with a will to conquer in the name of their great faith." [6] They did not impose their religion on conquered peoples, though they counted it foolish to think of a god like a man.

The Persian Empire extended from India on the east to the Danube on the west; and, of all the differing civilizations embraced in this vast territory,

[5] *The Cambridge Ancient History.*
[6] *The Stream of History*—Geoffrey Parsons.

only the Greek was never completely conquered. In contrast with the Assyrians and the later Romans, the Persians invariably conducted their wars with great humanity—respecting the temples and sparing the civilian population—and on the whole ruled the conquered territories with tolerance and generosity. Cyrus and Cambyses conquered and Darius solidified the empire and maintained what his predecessors had won. He built a great road-system, primarily for military purposes, which later was used for trade and commerce—a system that anticipated, even approached in excellence, the great road-system of the mighty Roman Empire.

These Persian rulers left the world a great idea, the idea of unity, the concept that all the world might be assembled under one rule. Throughout subsequent history one conqueror after another sought to follow that idea, only to fail, perhaps because of the selfishness of their aims. But out of these attempts there always resulted a mingling of peoples and an exchange of ideas, if nothing more.

As has been said, only Greece was never completely conquered by Persia. The democratic ideals of Athens and the warlike spirit of Sparta saved Europe from becoming a Persian satrapy. And the march of empire began moving westward. Alexander, to be sure, extended Greek civilization over most of the territory of the Persians and sighed for more worlds to conquer, but he reigned, only briefly, as an oriental despot and cannot be said to have ruled over a world empire.

Meanwhile, two little countries were playing an important part in the great world drama. In Palestine there was growing up a religion that would develop into a great church whose organization would one day replace the power of Imperial Rome. In Phœnicia had originated a people who came almost literally to live in the sea. Shipping and trade, mingled with a large element of adventure, carried them the length of the Mediterranean beyond Gibraltar; and, as they went, they spread ideas, interchanged wares, and brought the first taste of civilization to uncivilized peoples. We see them to-day as true advance agents of the march of progress.

This then, in brief, was the world-stage that History had set for the character whom William Shakespeare in all probability thought to be

"the noblest man
That ever lived in the tide of times."

We are now ready for the setting of the Roman scene.

The story of Rome begins with seven kings, and these seven kings, whose story the most diligent research has not been able to rescue wholly from the cloudland of tradition, were not gods but men, warring, irreligious men. Perhaps they were the first rulers of the world whose prerogatives did not begin with some sort of priestly duties. The Romans had scarcely any native mythology. However, they worshipped certain virtues, such as Valor, Truth, Good Faith, etc., and gradually accepted and adapted to their own use the gods of Greece. The story of the expulsion of the kings from Rome is too familiar to need, or to bear, repetition here. But this expulsion of the Tarquins was of great importance in the history of Rome, not only because it brought a change of government, but because it introduced an ideal that grew and perpetuated itself and eventually, as we shall find, caused the downfall of Julius Cæsar.

With the expulsion of the kings, the Roman Senate was reorganized with increased powers. Two consuls became the official heads of the government, serving for one year. They presided over the Senate and popular assemblies of the people, raised and commanded armies, organized newly conquered territory, and might even govern a province. Later the government of a province automatically followed the expiration of a term of consulship. The new government was called a Republic. It was not, however, a republic in the modern sense of rule by the people through elected representatives. The executive heads of the government were elected by vote of the patricians only. Later the people were able to secure representatives in the government called tribunes, but "there were lacking at Rome the very elements of democracy, an articulate commons, an organized will of the people." [7]

The Romans were by habit and instinct a fighting

[7] Stobart—*The Grandeur that was Rome.*

people. "From the earliest times they had inherited the custom of an annual summer campaign. . . . They were soldiers and nought else, and what are soldiers for but for fighting? . . . In the spring it was time to look about you and consider where and with whom you would begin to fight this year." [8] Rome's conquests, however, were not as deliberate in the early stages as those of most of her predecessors, but began in self-defense and self-preservation. Later, we are told, her struggle was "not for territorial aggrandisement but a struggle for wealth and even more for power, initiated by the imperialistic ambition of the Senate." [9]

Briefly to trace the development of Roman power: At the end of four centuries (to 338 B.C.) Rome found herself conqueror of Latium. Then in the comparatively short period of seventy-five years she had become ruler of Italy. In two centuries more she was mistress of the Mediterranean.

In her conquests Rome was relentless and unscrupulous, but she governed her provinces for the most part with broad-mindedness and generosity. This was due largely to an almost innate regard for law. As far back as the kings, custom had begun to take the form of law, and these laws were later reduced to a code and drawn up in the form of "Twelve Tables." "From that day to this," we are told, "whenever in the Western world men think about law or legislation, they think along Roman

---

[8] *Ibid.*   [9] *The Cambridge Ancient History.*

lines; there must be trial, evidence, proof; there must be no making of new laws by the judge; he is there to interpret and administer laws made by the sovereign, whether people, parliament or king, laws deliberately made with principles of justice at the core of them." [10] The priestly judges had made their own laws.

The Senate was in theory merely an advisory board which met only to give counsel to the magistrates, but its functions increased. It came to control the treasury, regulating all revenues and expenditures. It exercised judicial and executive powers and finally gained control of foreign policies, hearing and answering foreign embassies, and sending commissions of investigation and arbitration to foreign countries whenever disputes arose.[11] The Senate was composed exclusively of members of dominant families, families of wealth and nobility. Among their own number there was a consistent effort to keep any one member from obtaining a dangerous leadership. The Senate had allowed wealthy families to absorb large tracts of public lands that had been acquired by conquest. The first significant rebellion against this usurpation of power came from the Gracchi, tribunes of the people, who wished to use the public lands to create settlements for distressed citizens. (Later Julius Cæsar adopted and developed all that Gaius Gracchus did or proposed.)

[10] *The Ancient World*—Glover.
[11] See *The Cambridge Ancient History.*

Factions grew up in the Senate. Meanwhile the army had grown into a great power. Soldiering became a profession and, with the rival commanders Marius and Sulla, a new order came into being, an era when a Roman general, returning triumphant at the head of a powerful army, could take absolute control of affairs at home.

The Romans did not take naturally to the sea, but looked upon naval warfare as entirely secondary. "Through the whole period of the Republic they regarded a navy as potentially a necessity in case an emergency required it, not as one of the obvious means of defense to be continuously provided for in times of peace." [12] As a result of this laxness piracy grew up, became uncontrollable and soon came to infest every part of the Mediterranean. Pirates attacked sea-coast towns and carried their raids inland. They kidnapped Roman citizens, and among listed names of those captured we find that of Julius Cæsar.[13] But these pirate ships that swarmed everywhere carried slaves in great numbers, thus playing a part in the economic life of the times, and it was largely for this reason that they were tolerated for an incredible length of time.

All the while there was going on within the borders of the Roman world, which now extended from India on the east to Britain on the west, an exchange of luxuries and an interchange of philosophies, just

[12] Moore—*The Roman's World.*
[13] The story of his treatment of his captors is interesting reading.

as there had been a bartering of wares and a sharing of primitive thought from the very earliest movements of peoples into neighboring lands. Civilization up to the Roman expansion had meant Hellenism tinctured with Orientalism, for Greece and the Orient had acted and reacted upon each other for centuries. When Rome conquered Greece, it was the conquest of a barbarian people over a highly civilized people. There was no attempt to turn her authority into oppression, but Greece won a revenge for her political overthrow when her culture mastered her conquerors. Had Greek civilization come to Rome earlier, Stobart tells us,[14] "or been accepted more willingly, it might have done more to brighten the darker pages of Roman history." "It was their starved souls," this author continues, "empty of ideals, devoid of reasonable occupation for their leisure, or harmless use of their wealth, which rendered the aristocracy of Rome so utterly vulgar and debased." And again he tells us, "The truth is that Rome having grown rich was just beginning to grow civilized. It is the everlasting misfortune of Rome that events occurred in that order." However, there was never a wholesale foisting of Greek thought on an alien race. "From the first Rome chose what she would study, modified the traditions she received and thought out her ethics and politics to suit her own circumstances. . . . The Roman was a man of action and, if he reflected at all, he liked to think of the

[14] In *The Grandeur That Was Rome*.

practical business of life and the requirements of his state. . . . The Roman never quite renounced the shy suspicion that thinking might impede doing." [15]

The Empire-Republic, as it was called, had become too large and too complex to be ruled by the Senate, a Senate that had not only lost its morale but that had no understanding of the problems of the far-flung empire. Rome had inherited from Persia the idea of imperialistic government and from Greece the idea of government in a city-state. Now she seemed to be attempting to combine the two—and with ill success.

Great men, or rather influential men, rose in the Senate, only to give way to other influential men. Conspiracies were hatched, some of which were executed and some frustrated. Conquerors came home laden with the richest spoils of war the world had ever known, the world in which an empire was being ruled by a single city—and most of this wealth never found its way into the coffers of the state, but went to enrich private individuals. Indeed, the wealth of the world was concentrated in a few hands. Individuals were enormously wealthy and the state was bankrupt. The army had become professional and owed its allegiance to its commander, instead of to the state. The two political parties were the "Optimates" (or "best men"), the conservative nobility who sought to perpetuate the rule of the Senate, and the "Populares," the radical reformers composed

[15] *The Cambridge Ancient History,* Vol. VIII.

largely of the followers of the Gracchi, but with most of the wealth of business enlisted on their side. From early times Rome had turned to a dictator in periods of emergency, but now the dictator was the military High Command and the opposing parties each turned to its own High Command as a common practice. A biographer [16] sums up the situation thus briefly: "The position of the Senate was . . . anomalous and impotent. The power of the holders of the High Command was a return to barbarism. The whole of Rome's government had broken down, and what was to replace it? Could the people who had failed to rule a city rule the world? Had not Rome's success been her failure?"

This, in rapid review, was the condition of Rome when Julius Cæsar entered the scene. It would become his task to reorganize this broken world alone. Two other outstanding men of the time were Cicero and Pompey.

Marcus Tullius Cicero was one of the few honorable men of the Senate who tried to raise politics to a higher level. He was at the disadvantage of not having the dignity of ancestry. This handicap may have contributed seriously to a somewhat abnormal development, for he was at once shy, egotistical and often inconsistent. He wavered in loyalty between one party or another, but always stood for sound government. In spite of his lack of stability in the choice of friends, he was a power to be reckoned with in Rome,

[16] Buchan in *Augustus.*

and Cæsar, the shrewdest of judges of human nature, recognized his influence. He was steeped in the lore of the Twelve Tables and used all his matchless eloquence in expounding those laws. He had travelled and studied in Greece and, more than any one person, except the historian Polybius, he interpreted Greek thought to Rome. In addition to that, an historian [17] tells us, "He gave the West a philosophical language in which to think; for of all men in the West he created ideals in writing, of handling ideas of style and order, and so forth, so that whoever writes a good sentence in French or English to-day owes something to Cicero." His greatest act of heroism was accomplished during his consulship when he defeated the conspiracy of Catiline for a general massacre of senators and his own assassination. Ever after he thought and spoke of himself as the savior of Rome. In common with all the men of his generation, except Julius Cæsar, he lacked any clear vision of the future, and never saw the necessity for a strong central government.

Gnæus Pompey distinguished himself in the wars of Marius and Sulla and soon became a power in the military world. The pirate menace had grown to such proportions that at last it had to be dealt with. The pirates had for a long time bought off senatorial opposition, but when Rome began to starve for want of food from Sicily, Sardinia, and Africa, Pompey was given dictatorial powers by the people to rid the

[17] Glover in *The Ancient World.*

sea of these marauders and the country of a disgraceful scandal. Pompey could not be bribed by the pirates and, in forty days, he had cleared the Mediterranean of the "sea community" who, "led by highborn adventurers maintained out of their plunder a show of magnificence. The oars of the galleys of their commanders were plated with silver; their cabins were hung with gorgeous tapestries. They had bands of music to play at their triumphs." [18] Pompey accomplished his task by dividing the Mediterranean into thirteen districts and allotting a squadron to each under officers on whom he could thoroughly rely. The ease with which the task was accomplished "brought fresh disgrace on the Senate and fresh glory to the hero of the hour," Froude continues.

Some of Rome's conquered territories continued to revolt and to make trouble and Pompey was sent to reconquer Asia. Here, too, his success was dazzlingly rapid. It was at this time that he took Jerusalem by storm and entered the Holy of Holies, to find it empty, so far as Roman eyes could see. When the campaign was over, Egypt, of all the countries on the Mediterranean, was left partially independent. The conqueror returned personally poor, but filled the treasury to overflowing. His triumphal entry into Rome was magnificent. If he had been anything of a statesman, he might have been the first emperor of Rome, historians tell us. Cicero, who had greatly

[18] Froude.

feared that his own laurels might fade, was ill at ease until Pompey made his first speech in the Senate. Then the covering was off the feet of clay, and it became evident that Pompey was merely a man who had succeeded more through honesty than through any great military or other ability. One can easily believe the biographer, Froude, when he tells us that Cicero listened to Pompey's speech "with malicious satisfaction." But the two came to an amicable agreement on the agrarian laws which provided for Pompey's legionnaires. Cicero defended the measure in the Senate and Pompey, in the presence of that body, called him the "savior of the world." Cicero was delighted with the phrase and warmed to Pompey, thinking of him now as a convenient ally whom he hoped to control. But there was another person who was coming along "with the wind blowing full into his sails."

Gaius Julius Cæsar belonged to a patrician family. His father died when the boy was quite young. One of his boyhood heroes was his uncle (by marriage) Marius. Marius, a man of the people, had driven out the Germanic tribes that had been invading Italy to the extent that they had become a dangerous menace. It was he who had reorganized the citizen militia into a professional army. He had been made consul seven times. It is interesting to note that Cæsar's first political activities were directed against the vindictiveness of Sulla, his uncle's rival in the recent civil wars. The editors of *The Cambridge Ancient His-*

tory admit the possible connection between these first political activities and Cæsar's relationship to the house of Marius, but they relate Cæsar's policy more largely to the essential conciliatoriness of his political thought which rebelled against "blind excesses of partisanship." At any rate, he knew from early youth both the patrician and popular viewpoints and knew where he stood in relation to their respective causes.

As a young man Cæsar is said to have been given to "notorious moral laxity." It becomes the duty of the serious student to examine this charge and dispose of it as promptly as possible. The consensus of opinion among the historians of to-day is that most of the slander that gathered about Cæsar's name was entirely of political origin, the worst accusations having been made twenty years or more after the supposed commission of the guilty actions. These additional facts are brought out by historians and biographers: Cæsar found the drunken orgies of the male population so distressingly distasteful that, at banquets, where drunkenness and gluttony were the pastimes, he preferred and sought the company of the ladies. There were intellectual women in Rome and Cæsar found delight in conversation with them. That some of them were attracted to him or he to them would be foolish to question, but many of their husbands were his political enemies, and defaming a man's character was legitimate political ammunition in Rome. Divorce was common at the time. Men habitually divorced their wives to take younger ones.

They divorced wives for political reasons. They even made other marriages for them while they were pregnant. The story is told of one young woman in that condition who died as she entered the house of the new husband. Men gave their daughters, also, in marriage for political reasons. Cæsar, however, at nineteen, risked his own life by refusing to put away his wife at the command of Sulla. (He was married to her for sixteen years—until her death.) Pompey acquiesced and divorced his wife at Sulla's command. Cæsar had, over a period of years, four youthful wives. Divorce was easy for women to obtain from a husband who was untrue, but none of these wives ever made any attempt to divorce Cæsar. Perhaps the one love of his life was Servilia, the mother of Marcus Brutus. That Cæsar was the father of Brutus is altogether unlikely, since he was barely fifteen when the boy was born. A biographer [19] explains his unusual attachment to Brutus on the ground of Cæsar's deep regret at having been the cause of the divorce between the boy's parents. However, Servilia married again and it is uncertain how far Cæsar was able to take a father's place with Brutus. Certainly a rare friendship grew up between them.

A description of Cæsar's personal appearance and manners may with advantage be inserted here. The delineation is taken from Froude. "In person Cæsar was tall and slight. His features were more refined than was usual in Roman faces; the forehead was

[19] Fletcher Pratt in *Hail, Cæsar!*

the eyes dark gray like an eagle's, the neck extremely
thick and sinewy. His complexion was pale. . . .
His health was uniformly strong until the last year.
. . . He was a great bather, and scrupulously clean
in all his habits, abstemious in his food, and careless
of what it consisted, rarely or never touching wine,
and noting sobriety as the highest of qualities when
describing any new people. He was an athlete in
early life, admirable in all manly exercises, and especially in riding. In Gaul . . . he rode a remarkable
horse, which he had bred himself, and which would
let no one but Cæsar mount him. From his boyhood
it was observed of him that he was the truest of
friends, that he avoided quarrels, and was most easily
appeased when offended. In manner he was quiet
and gentlemanlike, with the natural courtesy of high
breeding." "On the whole," as Fowler concludes a
similar description, "we may picture him to ourselves
as a man the dignity of whose bodily presence was in
due proportion to the greatness of his mental powers."

Another charge of which the student of Shakespeare will wish to clear the name of Cæsar is that of
participation in the great Catilinian conspiracy. It
was claimed that he tried to save the lives of the
guilty persons, but the modern historian, reading the
records without prejudice, finds that, "What he actually did was to urge the Senate not to lose its head
and do an unconstitutional and unwise thing in its
fright." [20] The author quoted continues, "There is

[20] Glover.

nothing so obviously unpatriotic, some people always think, as to keep calm and sensible in a national emergency." [21] "No conspiracy is so puzzling as this of Catilina" another historian [22] tells us. He continues, "We cannot see that he [Catilina] pretended to belong to any of the existing parties of Rome. He was not a conservative. He was attacked and destroyed by a combination of the Optimates. He was not a liberal; his principal supporters were the friends and supporters of Sulla, who hated the Marian party. . . . Probably Catilina desired a dictatorship for himself like that of Sulla, for purely selfish ends, to enrich himself and his adherents by a new proscription. That the sympathy of Cæsar can have been enlisted in behalf of such a scheme is a moral impossibility." *The Cambridge Ancient History* says,[23] "Though Cicero in later years roundly incriminated Cæsar, it is practically certain that he never possessed any valid evidence against him, and that such evidence did not exist."

No detailed discussion of the local politics in which Cæsar played a part is necessary in this place. On the whole his sympathies were with the popular cause, and he became the leader of the popular party, but he could never be coerced by either side into joining any rash venture. He had prepared himself for his work as an active member of his political world

[21] Fowler gives the substance of his speech in the Senate and tells us that shorthand was used in the debate.

[22] Baring-Gould.

[23] Vol. IX—p. 503.

by studying under a Greek master at Rhodes, and was accounted to be second only to Cicero in oratory. When he became consul it was with a colleague of the senatorial party who was hostile enough to oppose him at every turn. Cæsar overrode all the other's vetoes, and the wags said the two consuls that year were Julius and Cæsar. Fowler tells us, "It is true that such influence as the Senate possessed had been undermined during Cæsar's consulship." Froude goes further and says, "The consulship of Cæsar was the last chance for the Roman aristocracy."

The reign of lawlessness which followed the wholesale murder of the participants in the Catilinian conspiracy turned the minds of the people to Pompey, who was returning from the reconquest of Asia. Cicero was temporarily under a cloud—a reaction had set in against the triumph and "glory of that September day" and he was forbidden to deliver a speech in the Senate on the ground that he had put Roman citizens to death without a hearing. Both the Optimates and the Populares dreaded the power of Pompey—in case it should be enlisted on the other side. The people's demand for Pompey, if Pompey allied himself with them, would place the state's two strongest men on the side of the populace, Cæsar with the people strongly behind him and Pompey with a powerful army at his back. Obviously the Senate would oppose any such combination. Together they, Cæsar and Pompey, could overthrow the government and abolish the Senate. The Senators trumped up a story about Cæsar and Pompey's wife and privately sent word to Pompey that his friend had taken advantage of his absence. On the strength of this gossip Pompey divorced his wife before his return, but he must later have been convinced of the falsity of the report because soon after his return he was married to Cæsar's daughter, Julia.[24] The editors of *The Cambridge Ancient History* deal with the matter as follows: "He [Cæsar] came under suspicion of having been a partner in the unfaithfulness of Pompey's third wife. But for all these ill turns Pompey bore him no lasting resentment." Again a comment on this aspect of Cæsar's life seems worthy of consideration—this time from Froude: "It would be idle to believe that Cæsar was particularly virtuous. He was a man of the world living in an age as corrupt as has ever been known. It would be equally idle to assume that all the ink blots thrown upon him were certainly deserved because we find them in books which we call classical. Proof deserving to be called proof there is none; and the only real evidence is the town talk of a society which feared and hated Cæsar and was glad of every pretext to injure him when alive or to discredit him after his death. Similar stories have been spread, are spread, and will be spread of every man who raises himself a few inches above the level of his fellows." When scandal touched the name of Cæsar's wife, Pompeia, he divorced her

[24] Sometimes these young Roman girls had a genuine admiration for the "great" men they married, and Julia seems genuinely to have loved Pompey.

and when asked his reason answered haughtily, "Cæsar's wife must be above suspicion." On this Baring-Gould remarks, "It seems impossible to believe that Cæsar would have divorced Pompeia for infidelity knowing himself to be false to her." Of interest, also, is the view of R. H. Towner,[25] who accounts for Cæsar's genius on the ground of the sexual coldness of the maternal strain.

Cæsar's first military experience was in Spain, after his consulship, where he was sent to complete Pompey's work of conquest and settle the finances of the country, and there he is thought to have discovered the latent military ability that soon led him to undertake the campaigns in Gaul.

In 58 B.C. Cæsar was given the governorship of Cisalpine Gaul and Illyricum by the people, and in the following year the Senate conferred on him the governorship of Transalpine Gaul. As to Cæsar's object in seeking the governorship of these provinces, it has been frequently claimed that his purpose was to raise and train a powerful army to support his political ambitions. However, the more sympathetic historians stress the fact that he alone recognized the danger that menaced Rome from the north. Baring-Gould tells us, "Cæsar required military power for his party purposes, but Cæsar did not subjugate Gaul as a party man. It was for Rome a political necessity to meet, and plant a dam against, the perpetually threatening invasion of the Germans so as to assure

[25] In *The Philosophy of Civilization.*

peace to the Roman world." Cæsar was comparatively inexperienced in military command and, as
The Cambridge Ancient History puts it, "It is not
unlikely that the Senate banked on his essaying a task
beyond his powers and in this spirit put out a liberal
length of rope for Cæsar to hang himself." At least
they were to be rid of him for five years.

Cæsar was now forty-three years of age, rather
late, one might think, for beginning a military career,
but his abstemious habits had left his wiry strength
unimpaired. His men were more completely trained
than any army that had ever taken the field, perhaps
one could say than any that *has* ever taken the field.
They were trained as engineers, as woodsmen, and
as shipbuilders. It has been said that their campaigns were fought with spade, pick-axe, and hatchet
more than with sword and lance. Above all, Cæsar
was in complete command and there could be no
instructions from Rome. Cicero, who had had some
military experience, declined to go as Cæsar's first
lieutenant, and Cæsar chose Labienus for that office.
The student should make a mental note of Labienus.
He will hear of him again. Four years later Mark
Antony joined Cæsar's staff in Gaul. A year after
that Trebonius, also a character in the play, joined
Cæsar as one of his principal officers. The Cicero
mentioned in the *Commentaries* was a brother of
Tullus.

Cæsar spent nine years in Gaul, going into winter
quarters in Cisalpine Gaul. In Cisalpine Gaul he

found all that was best in Italy. Fowler tells us that "Cisalpine Gaul had long been peculiarly attached to Cæsar himself and the democratic party . . . Catullus, Virgil, Livy, and the elder and younger Pliny, among many others, were all natives of this district, which long continued to present in its purity and simplicity of manners, as well as in the health and vigour of its culture, a marked contrast to the selfish, and worn-out population of the capital."

At the end of nine years Cæsar crossed the Rubicon. In those nine years, as Glover tells us, he "learned to handle great issues with a freedom he would never have learned in the Roman streets." This author continues: "The great open spaces change a man's thoughts and a new world sends him a new man back to an old world. The Cæsar who crosses the Rubicon is ready for the greatest tasks and he is not afraid of them . . . Night by night, day by day Cæsar in Gaul was handling great problems; the distances, the shape of the country, the spirit of the people, all had to be realized; his tools, not altogether strange to him, had to be realized as well. The handling of great armies, all that strategy and tactics mean, was part of his task: where should he send his troops, how should he place them? . . . He had to weld his forces and make them his own; and this he did. When Cæsar leaves Gaul he takes with him an experience wrought into his nature that made it over again; he has had to think on a great scale; he has done it and he knows he can do it again. Pompey no doubt had had some such experience in Spain; but experience means more to genius. By the time they were both dead it was plain that Pompey was one of Rome's capable generals and Cæsar was one of the world's greatest soldiers. Could his genius have grown to such greatness without the nine years' discipline in Gaul?" As to what Cæsar accomplished of world consequence, this historian tells us further: "Cæsar (to speak in an abrupt way) turned Gaul into France, and that matters to all mankind, and, more than we sometimes realize, Gaul made Cæsar —the Cæsar who built the framework that saved Greek and Latin civilization, of which we are heirs every one of us, however forgetful or ungrateful."

In his mention of the great open spaces and their effect on Cæsar, the historian just quoted more than hints at a spiritual development that we shall find suggested throughout Shakespeare's play. And following that hint along with a few telling facts given us by the biographers, we can picture Cæsar as he slept night after night under the summer skies watching and studying the stars. We may be confident of our ground in suggesting this study since he made friends with the Druids who are known to have been astronomers. He mentions them often in his *Commentaries,* as when he says, "They likewise discuss and impart to the youth many things respecting the stars and their motion, respecting the extent of the world and of our earth, respecting the nature of things, respecting the power and the majesty of the immortal gods." Surely we must believe that there in the forests of Gaul something of the longing described by Matthew Arnold [26] must have come to him as he, too, traced the progress of the stars and saw how

> "self-poised they live nor pine
> with noting
> All the fever of some differing soul."

The senators at home were differing souls and surely he must have forgotten, or learned to disregard, all the ugliness of the fevered life at Rome. Unaided by Persian, Greek, or Hebrew thought, he must have found the Soul of the Universe, a God who was not like a man. The experience was one to make his soul grow "vast" like the heavenly bodies—to continue with the thought of Matthew Arnold. In keeping with this thought we find one of his biographers [27] saying, "He moved through life calm and irresistible like a force of nature." And another [28] says, "He moved about the globe like a fire . . . conducting himself like one who believes that he has a divine mission and that the gods will not recall him till it is fulfilled." Only a few of those who were with him in Gaul would have any comprehension of this change, and Rome would never understand. Once back in Rome some of the old habits of thought might persist. He would even consult the oracles—so long

---

[26] In the poem, *Self-Dependence.*
[27] Froude.
[28] John Buchan in *Julius Cæsar.*

does it take aspiring but unstable man to throw off the shackles of inherited fear.

Many times on those nights under the stars his thoughts must have trailed off to scenes and people at home, to the Senate, to Virgilia, to Brutus. He had watched the boy grow into manhood with feelings of pride. He had helped to train the fine mind of Brutus and to mold his character. He had come to love him as a son—but he knew that Brutus was not practical enough to carry on the great work that was hourly taking form in his mind. But Brutus would understand, Brutus with his great love for Rome. There was comfort in the thought of Brutus' understanding. Antony? No. Antony's character had been virtually remade under his influence (and Cæsar's reputation had suffered by the contact with Antony), but was Antony the one to carry on? No. Of all his nephews Augustus was the most promising. He must see more of that boy. But if he had a son of his own—sleep must have come many times on the thought of the son he still might have.

Now this man was going back with a new way of life for Rome. He had written to private friends and his agents, Balbus and Oppus, stating "in explicit terms his determination not to imitate the cruelty of Sulla and others in previous civil wars. My method of conquest shall be a new one; I will fortify myself with compassion and generosity." [29] A little later his nephew, Augustus, heard him explain the practical

[29] Fowler. The author tells us this note is still preserved.

parts of the plan "during late watches in the camp in his quiet reedy voice when the eyes in the lean face seemed in the lamplight to have the masterful luminosity of Jove's eagle." [30] To continue with Buchan the description of the plan, "Law and order must be restored. The empire must be governed and there must be a center of power. The Roman world required a single administrative system. This could not be given by the people, for the mob could not govern. It could not be given by the Senate which had shown itself in the highest degree incompetent, and in any case had no means of holding the soldiers' loyalty. Only a man could meet the need, a man who had the undivided allegiance of the army, and that the only army. . . . It was a new kind of empire. Something had been drawn from the dreams of Alexander but for the most part it was the creation of his own profound and audacious mind. There were to be wide local liberties. He proposed to decentralize, to establish local government in Italy as the beginning of a world-wide system of free municipalities. Rome was to be only the greatest among many great autonomous cities. There was to be a universal Roman nation, not a city with a host of servile provinces, and citizenship in it should be open to all who were worthy."

Even this brief sketch of Cæsar's great ideal should convince the modern reader that it is not to be confused with the plans of modern dictators, though he

[30] Buchan in *Augustus*.

is often referred to as a dictator. Somewhat along this line of thought a modern historian,[31] though dealing with a different period, says, "Dante wrote to prove that sovereignty exists to preserve for all men spiritual freedom, a truth that is still imperfectly realized; and that there are divine laws which a secular power is incompetent to administer—a truth that the totalitarian state denies." Considering these things, one wonders whether Julius Cæsar may not have been the first and the only man who might have been both priest and sovereign of the world.

But we seem to have passed far beyond the Rubicon and must go back. The political situation leading to Cæsar's return was briefly as follows. His second term as governor of Gaul was drawing to a close. He had been promised a consulship on his return. His enemies in the Senate were deeply opposed to his coming into power. He had made laws during his first consulship which they had not been able to repeal. He was more powerful now with an army behind him, and, therefore, more dangerous. He had become adored by his legions and the people of Italy. "He was the idol of the hour. No fault could be found with his administration. His wars had paid for themselves." [32] The Senate knew well by this time that Cæsar had not gone through the campaigns in Gaul merely to come back and be in control of local politics. As Froude puts it, "A lunatic might

[31] H. Maynard Smith—*Pre-Reformation England*.
[32] Froude.

have entertained such a scheme, but not Cæsar." The Senate now recognized him as a reformer and their selfishness did not wish to see the state reformed. The only national spirit left was to be found among Cæsar's legionnaires. If these men and their families could be given farms in Italy and the provinces the country might still be saved. This was part of Cæsar's reformation plan and it did not meet the Senate's approval. Also, Cæsar had added a rich province to his country and the Senators were envious of his popularity with the Gauls, who had become reconciled to Roman rule under Cæsar.

The Senate turned to Pompey. After all, Pompey was only a little man compared with Cæsar, and Cæsar's success had been too much for him. The death of his wife, Julia, had broken the last personal tie that bound the two men.[33] Pompey was early won over to the senatorial interests. The Senate placed two of Cæsar's legions at Pompey's disposal, under the pretense of using them in a campaign against the Parthians. Cæsar saw through the trick, but sent the legions demanded of him (one of which had been earlier lent him by Pompey). Excuses were then made for bringing Cæsar's governorship to an end six months earlier than the appointed date of expiration. Thus he would not be permitted to step from one public office to another, but would become a private citizen for six months, during which time

[33] The news of his daughter's death was found in the post that awaited Cæsar on his return from England.

he would be at the mercy of his enemies. Pompey with his two legions could effectively stop any popular movement in favor of Cæsar. Cæsar made a countermove by managing the election of Mark Antony as tribune, and he probably bought off the Senate's elected tribune (young Cato) by paying his debts. At least Cato deserted the Senate and stood with Antony for the interests of Cæsar. This threw the Senate into a turmoil and Pompey wavered. The Senate then successfully bribed Labiènus, Cæsar's most trusted officer. Following the biographer Froude once more, we find this explanation: "Labienus had made a vast fortune in the war. He perhaps thought, as other distinguished officers have done, that he was the person who had won the victories; that without him Cæsar, who had been so much praised and glorified, would have been nothing; and that he at least was entitled to an equal share of the honors and rewards that might be coming; while if Cæsar was to be disgraced, he might have the whole recompense for himself." Cæsar refused to believe in his treachery. Messengers who had been sent to Cæsar returned with no reply from Cæsar but with the report that Cæsar's troops were worn out, discontented and disloyal—this in all probability from Labienus. Then Cæsar sent the Senate three alternatives, thus summarized by Froude: "First, that the agreement already made might stand, and that he might be nominated, in his absence, for the consulship; or that when he left his army, Pompey should disband his

Italian legions; or, lastly, that he should hand over Transalpine Gaul to his successor with eight of his legions, himself keeping the north of Italy and Illyria with two until the election." The Senate voted that Cæsar must dismiss his army by a certain date or be declared an enemy of the state. Mark Antony and another tribune vetoed the measure but to no avail. The Senate appointed Cæsar's most inveterate enemy to displace him and made Pompey Commander-in-Chief of a general levy of Italian soldiers, giving him the key to the treasury. Mark Antony and two other tribunes fled to Cæsar disguised as peasants. Cæsar, when he heard of the Senate's action, addressed his soldiers, telling them what the Senate had done and reviewing all that he and they had accomplished in Gaul. With the exception of one man the soldiers declared for Cæsar—and Labienus left to join Pompey. Cæsar crossed the Rubicon into Italy and the action was equivalent to a declaration of war on the Senate, though Cæsar was still ready to make peace. For a proconsul to pass beyond the boundary of his province was high treason to the state. Here, at the risk of destroying a cherished mental picture of some "Dear Reader" we must quote, again from Froude, as follows: "The vision of the Rubicon with the celebrated saying that 'the die is cast' is unauthenticated and not at all consistent with Cæsar's character."

When the Senators learned that Cæsar had entered Italy with an army, they fled from Rome in a panic, leaving their wives, children, and property behind.

Pompey, their appointed protector, seems to have failed them and did not know his own mind. Cæsar and Antony, taking separate routes, marched toward Rome, their army increasing as they passed through the country. All Italy was with Cæsar, but "the east with its treasures, its fleets, its millions of men, this was Pompey's, heart and soul. The sea was Pompey's." [34] The contest was narrowing down to a personal issue between Cæsar and Pompey. Cæsar wrote to Pompey, begging for an interview and proposing that they should both disarm, that Pompey should proceed to Spain and that he himself should give up his imperium and go to Rome to stand for the consulship. He believed that he could reason with Pompey if he could get an interview. But Pompey decided to leave Italy and to fight, if necessary, in the East, which was his old camping-ground. "His vanity had been so deeply wounded", Buchan tells us, "that he was ready to war to the uttermost." Cæsar gave up hope of an interview for the present and attempted to work out some kind of interim government with the senators who had not fled the city. The consuls were absent and the Senate was convened by Mark Antony and another tribune. It had been ten years since Cæsar had appeared in the Senate, and the few senators who were present beheld a new man. There was a rare, new gentleness in his manner and speech which was mistaken for timidity or affectation. He proposed terms for peace and asked for the consul-

[34] Froude.

ship. Spain had revolted to Pompey and Rome was between two fires. Cæsar took command of the situation at home by appointing Lepidus, the prætor, as chief officer in Rome and placing Antony in command of the Italian troops. He himself then went to quell the uprising in Spain. In forty days he succeeded "by taking risks which would have been insane except for a general who had a veteran army in which he could implicitly trust." [35]   On his return to Rome he was made dictator in order to hold the consular elections. He held the post for eleven days —until he could be duly nominated for the consulship. Cæsar was now in control of Italy, Spain, Gaul, Sardinia, and Sicily. Having obtained the consulship he then went in search of Pompey, hoping to come to some sort of reasonable agreement. Pompey, meanwhile, had raised an army and was in command of a magnificent fleet. He was planning to reconquer Italy in the spring. Cæsar met him at Dyrrhachium. The details of a Roman battle are no longer interesting. Briefly, Cæsar was defeated for the second time in his career. Then came Pharsalia.

At Pharsalia, with Cæsar commanding the right wing and Mark Antony the left of an army inferior in numbers, Pompey was brought down in defeat. And with Pompey the cause of the corrupt Roman Senate met defeat, a defeat which came largely through the misrepresentations of Labienus, whose services they had purchased. On this single battle-

[35] Buchan.

field, as Fowler tells us, the contending forces of a world-wide revolution were focused. This author continues: "On one side the disunion, selfishness, and pride of the last survivors of an ancient oligarchy, speculating before the event on the wealth or office that victory was to bring them; on the other the absolute command of a single man, whose clear mental vision was entirely occupied with the facts and issues that lay before him that day. . . . With Pompeius was the spirit of the past, and his failure did but answer to the failure of a decaying world; with Cæsar was the spirit of the future, and his victory marks the moment when humanity could once more start hopefully upon a new line of progress."

At Pharsalia Marcus Brutus had fought on the side of Pompey because he believed in the rightness of Pompey's cause. Before the battle Cæsar had given instructions that Brutus should be unharmed. When the battle was over Brutus brought a companion, Caius Cassius, before Cæsar, begging for his pardon. It was granted. This was a popular story and its authenticity has been questioned. However, the student of Shakespeare needs only to remember that Brutus and Cassius had been very close friends.

After the battle Cæsar followed Pompey to Egypt, still hoping to patch up some kind of reconciliation, and on landing at Alexandria was met with the news that Pompey had been murdered by order of the young king. Buchan's comment on Pompey's death is: It was "a melancholy end for a just man who had stumbled upon a destiny too great for him." And Froude says, "He was a weak, good man whom accident had thrust into a place to which he was unequal; and ignorant of himself, and unwilling to part with his imaginary greatness, he was flung down with careless cruelty by the forces that were dividing the world."

Egypt was in confusion, and it was in connection with a tangled political situation that Cæsar met Cleopatra. Here again we are confronted with a controversial subject—that of the outcome of that meeting. Four quotations on the subject, from the highest sources, will dispose of the matter for our purposes. "Cleopatra had a right to be heard if Cæsar was to be judge, and she contrived to reach the city and to find a boatman to take her to him. She came, saw and conquered. To the military difficulties of withdrawal in the face of the Egyptian army was added the fact that Cæsar no longer wished to go. He was past fifty but he retained an imperious susceptibility which evoked the admiration of his soldiers. Cleopatra was twenty-two, as ambitious and high-mettled as Cæsar himself, a woman whom he would find it easy to understand and admire as well as love. The path of safety and self-denying statesmanship led away from Alexandria, but only those who underrate the daring and the egotism of Cæsar will be surprised that he did not follow it." [36]

"The conqueror of Pompey was besieged all win-

[36] *The Cambridge Ancient History.*

ter in Alexandria, and it was not until March, 47, that he was relieved by young Mithridates . . . and Cleopatra and her younger brother were placed on the throne. To that winter belong strange tales. He had an affair with Cleopatra and delayed in Egypt three months . . . though the affairs of the world clamoured for his attention. He is said to have sailed with her far up the Nile . . . Over a man, too, who had led the life of the camp, the wit and beauty of that supreme enchantress may have cast a spell.[37] She had a son during the year which she fathered upon him. . . . Cæsar's friends disbelieved the tale of Cæsarion's paternity and later ages are free to decide as they please." [38]

"But had there been any amour carried on by Cæsar with Cleopatra, there almost certainly would be a trace of such a report in the letters of Cicero to Atticus, for he picked up and detailed to his friend all the gossip of the city. . . . Had Cæsarion been the child of the great dictator, we may be sure Cæsar would have mentioned him in his will and left him to the protection of the Roman people. But he did not allude to him by a word, and it was regarded as a singular and pointed slight for a Roman not to leave something to every friend and kinsman. . . . Every kind of malevolent report that could prejudice Cæsar with the multitude was diligently spread. It was said that he was going to abandon Rome and rebuild Troy

[37] But does this author recall that he left the life of the camp and wintered in the cultured atmosphere of Cisalpine Gaul?

[38] John Buchan in *Julius Cæsar.*

and make that the capital of the world, because the sacred Julian race was supposed to come from thence." [39]

"Roman scandal discovered afterwards that Cæsar had been fascinated by the charms of Cleopatra, and allowed his politics to be influenced by a love affair. Roman fashionable society hated Cæsar, and any carrion was welcome to them which would taint his reputation. Cleopatra herself favored the story, and afterwards produced a child which she named Cæsarion. . . . An amour with Cleopatra may have been an accident of his presence in Alexandria. But to suppose that such a person as Cæsar, with the concerns of the world upon his hands, would have allowed his public action to be governed by a connection with a loose girl of sixteen is to make too large a demand upon human credulity. . . . The report proves nothing, but whether true or false it was certain to arise. The *salons* of Rome, like the *salons* of Paris, took their revenge on greatness by soiling it with filth; and happily Suetonius, the chief authority for the scandal, couples it with a story which is demonstrably false. He says that Cæsar made a long expedition with Cleopatra in a barge upon the Nile, that he was so fascinated with her that he wished to extend his voyage to Ethiopia, and was prevented only by the refusal of his army to follow him. The details of Cæsar's stay at Alexandria, so minutely given by Hirtius, show that there was not a moment

[39] Baring-Gould.

when such an expedition could have been contemplated. During a greater part of the time he was blockaded in the palace. Immediately after the insurrection was put down, he was obliged to hurry off on matters of instant and urgent moment. . . . Of the time in which legend describes him as abandoned to his love for Cleopatra, there was hardly an hour of either day or night in which he was not fighting for his life. . . . Cleopatra is said to have joined Cæsar at Rome after his return from Spain and to have resided openly with him as his mistress. Supposing that she did come to Rome, it is still certain that Calpurnia was in Cæsar's house when he was killed. Cleopatra must have been Calpurnia's guest as well as her husband's, and her presence, however commented upon in society, could not possibly have borne the avowed complexion which tradition assigned to it. On the other hand, it is quite intelligible that the young Queen of Egypt, who owed her position to Cæsar, might have come, as other princes came, on a visit of courtesy, and that Cæsar, after their acquaintance in Alexandria, should invite her to stay with him. But was Cleopatra at Rome at all? The only real evidence for her presence there is to be found in a few words of Cicero. . . . 'I am not sorry to hear of the flight of the queen.' There is nothing to show that the 'queen' was the Egyptian queen. Granting that the word Egyptian is to be understood, Cicero may have referred to Arsinoe, who was called queen as well as her sister, and had been sent to Rome to be shown in Cæsar's triumph. But enough and too much of this miserable subject. Men will continue to form their own opinions about it not upon evidence, but according to their preconceived notions of what is probable or improbable." [40]

On his return to Rome after the conquest of Pompey, Cæsar was made dictator for a year. He pardoned the followers of Pompey and they accepted his leadership with abject servility. In their hearts they knew that it was the Senate and Pompey that had provoked the war and that Cæsar had to defend himself. He refused to punish his political opponents. He killed no one and deprived no one of his property. But, as Fowler puts it, the "deadly foes alike to Cæsar and to reason, . . . refused to abide by the decrees of fate, and to allow the great conqueror the chance of being also a great leader."

Labienus had joined the sons of Pompey in Spain and these irreconcilables were strong at sea. They must be dealt with before Rome could have peace. Weary of battle, Cæsar once more went on a campaign against the enemies of Rome. "It was an enterprise to which even the Roman conservatives wished him well. They had no desire to come under the

[40] Froude.

Fowler inclines to the belief in an "affair" but does not cover the situation broadly and we find no brief quotable passages. Fletcher Pratt assures us that there was no "girl fever", that peculiar malady that attacks many men in their fifties (and becomes epidemic in some ages) but that the association was largely intellectual and based on political necessity. There was, therefore, according to this author, "no evidence of any decline in Cæsar's intellect or energy."

tyranny of a savage like young Pompey." [41] At the battle of Munda Labienus and young Pompey were killed and their cause lost. Of this war Fowler tells us, "No war was ever more unreasonable, or more cruelly waged, than this fresh outbreak by the Pompeian party; it was a war of darkness against light." Cæsar was accompanied on the journey by his nephew Augustus, a young boy approaching his eighteenth birthday. With them in the carriage was Decimus Brutus, a man whom Cæsar liked and trusted. He comes into Shakespeare's play as Decius Brutus. [42]

After his return from Spain Cæsar was again made dictator, probably without definite limit of time. According to Fowler, "There was nothing to show that they [the prerogatives given] were intended to be permanent; even the unlimited dictatorship was probably understood as provisional only, being . . . a bestowal of power to build up a constitution, and in no sense a part of the constitution itself. That ancient office had always been a temporary expedient —a brief reversion to kingship—in order to tide over a present difficulty. As such it was used now; for a permanent dictatorship was to a Roman a contradiction in terms." When he was made dictator the Senate took an oath to guard his person. Later he

[41] Buchan.
[42] It is thought that Plutarch confused Decimus with Marcus Brutus and that Shakespeare fell into his error. However, the two personalities have been so long differentiated in the play that no attempt is made now to untangle the error.

accepted the title of Imperator, an office that united civil and military command. He was officially deified and a temple was dedicated to him in the Forum. The deification of rulers had begun in Greece. Deification was a way of legalizing absolutism and a man so uplifted above his fellows was looked upon as a god among men.[43] "But by whatever flattering name they called him they knew that he alone held the reins; he alone was able to hold them."[44] They knew they could not escape his reforms, and their resentment grew. Cæsar on his part wished only to be the guardian of the Roman interests, but he was becoming weary of it all—weary of the ill-concealed treachery, and the distrust, and the misunderstanding—this man who had never rested, whose almost superhuman physical strength had for years met and conquered what were to others insurmountable difficulties.

So we come to the fifteenth day of February in the year 44 B.C., the day on which William Shakespeare has chosen to open his play.

In the early part of this month of February, Cæsar had been made dictator for life, "a serious step," Fowler tells us, "because it put an entirely new meaning on the old republican institution. He now began to allow the image of his head to be placed on the coinage. This held no precedent in Roman history, but it had always been, in the empires of the East,

---

[43] See *The Cambridge Ancient History*. Vol. VII.
[44] Froude.

the special prerogative of the monarch. He allowed his statue to be added to those of the seven kings of Rome on the Capitol. He appeared on public occasions in the purple triumphal dress." And again from Fowler we find, "But he was on a far higher pinnacle of personal power than any one man can safely hold, who has won it by force of arms in a state corrupt and diseased. It was not his work that was recognized and lauded but his power."

On that fifteenth day of February came the celebration of the Lupercal, which event Shakespeare has chosen to combine with the triumph that had occurred earlier when Cæsar returned from Spain. The Lupercalia is explained in any good school edition of the play. As the scene opens on a street in Rome, Flavius and Marullus, the tribunes, are reprimanding a group of idle workmen and attempting to drive them off the streets. The questions of the Tribunes and the glib, quibbling answers of the workmen need no explanation except the mention of neat's leather. This was an Elizabethan leather, ox-hide, which Englishmen were urged to use in preference to imported leathers, and the expression "as proper a man as ever trod upon neat's leather" came to mean as good a man as ever walked.[45]

The Second Commoner at last answers the Tribune seriously and courteously that they are making a holiday to see Cæsar and rejoice at his triumphs over the sons of Pompey. Marullus begins to ha-

[45] See *Costume in Elizabethan Drama*—Linthicum.

rangue the crowd, asking why they should rejoice. He asks what spoils ("conquests") Cæsar has brought home and what prisoners of war have followed his chariot wheels. Cæsar's triumphs were extravagant enough (though on his return from Africa he permitted no captive Roman to follow his car) but perhaps the Tribune wishes here to minimize these triumphs in comparison with the gorgeous triumph of Pompey. Whether such pomp as Cæsar permitted was displayed for the purpose of impressing his power upon the Roman people (and they could understand it in no other way) or whether he had succumbed to this outward show of magnificence cannot at this late time be definitely decided.

Marullus begins to scold the workmen, calling them blocks and stones and worse than senseless things. He shames them for their hardness of heart and their cruelty. By the time the sentence is finished we know that he is a follower of Pompey. He reminds them of the many times they climbed up to walls and battlements, to towers and windows, even to the tops of chimneys, with their infants in their arms, and sat the livelong day waiting patiently to see the great Pompey coming home in triumph; and when they finally caught sight of the conqueror's chariot they shouted together, making such a volume of sound that the river Tiber trembled on hearing the reverberation ("replication") of their shouts within the hollow confines of her shores. Now, he continues, they have put on their best attire and are making a holiday to strew flowers in the path of Cæsar who has come home in triumph over Pompey's sons, one of whom was killed in battle ("Pompey's blood"). Marullus tells the idlers to get themselves home, admonishing them to fall upon their knees and pray to the gods to prevent the plague which is the natural result of, or punishment for, such ingratitude.

Flavius speaks and tells the "good countrymen" that because of their shortcomings, in thus honoring Cæsar, they must now go and assemble all the poor men of their sort, bring them to the Tiber and there all of them weep into the channel until the lowest levels of the stream are no more but have risen and all but overflowed the banks. The people move away and Flavius turns to Marullus. The second word in the next sentence has been changed to "whether" by some editors. The word in the *First Folio* is "where." [46] Retaining the word "where", the meaning seems to be, See, or do you notice, that wherever, or whenever, their base natures are unmoved or uninspired, as by the stimulating sight of a triumph, they are ready to vanish in tongue-tied guiltiness. In other words, Flavius gives a picture of these people slinking away like natural-born criminals, quite unlike the appearance they would make when inspired by the accomplishment or triumphal display of some leader. The word "whether" used here might

[46] Copies of the *Folio* differ in some words. Even if found, the "whe'er" seems more likely to mean "whenever" than "whether."

be a suggestion that Marullus follow these workmen, at the request of Flavius, to see whether their base metal has been moved by his speech. Flavius suggests that they go different ways and dismantle the images (statues of Cæsar) as they go, disrobe them of the decorations with which they have been ceremoniously or pompously decked. Marullus questions their right to do this, reminding his companion that it is a holiday. Flavius takes the responsibility of the action and says the holiday makes no difference. No statue may be hung with garlands or crowns ("trophies") [47] he declares. He will go about, he continues, and drive the vulgar from the streets and Marullus must do likewise. Cæsar's growing feathers, he adds, if plucked in time will enable him to fly only an ordinary height; otherwise he will soar above the plane on which other men get their view of life (not literally out of sight) and will keep them all in servile fear.

[47] See "trophy"—*Onions' Glossary.*

ACT I—SCENE II

In February, 44 B.C., Julius Cæsar was waiting for the breaking up of wintry weather to start on a campaign into Parthia, which was now the only unconquered territory in the Roman world. The Parthians were celebrated for their skill with the bow and arrow and many Romans had gone down before the famous Parthian darts. The campaign was likely to be a long one, and many things might happen before his return; so he made a new will. He named as his first heir the son that Calpurnia might bear him during his absence.[1] He was now fifty-six, his thought may have been running, as he made his will, but once the hardships of the Parthian campaign were over he might hope to live twenty years or more, and twenty years is long enough to instill one's ideals into the mind of a boy. He knew what his influence had done for others—yes, there might still be time to train as his successor the boy who would be his own son.[2]

It is on this wistful note of son-longing that Shakespeare introduces him into the play. "Calpurnia!", he calls to his young wife. The voice is clear and

[1] There being no son, his great-nephew, Octavius, became his heir. Decimus Brutus was the next largest inheritor.

[2] To be sure, there are historians who believe that he wished only to establish a dynasty.

vibrating, but not deep. Casca, in a bigger, rumbling voice, orders the people to be quiet and hear Cæsar speak. Cæsar calls his wife's name again and she comes before him. He bids her stand in the way of Antony as he runs, then, calling to Antony, he reminds him to touch Calpurnia with the leather thong he is carrying. A part of the ceremony of celebrating the Lupercal was the sacrifice of a goat, or goats, in honor of Romulus and Remus, the traditional founders of the city, and the old mother wolf. The skin of these animals was then cut into strips for the runners' thongs. The runners playfully tapped the bystanders with these thongs as part of the sport of the day. The superstition had grown up that a woman thus touched who was with child would have a safe delivery, and a barren woman would become pregnant. Antony assures Cæsar that he will remember, adding, "When Cæsar says, 'do this', it is performed." Cæsar orders the race to begin and tells the runners to leave out no part of the ceremony— obviously observing all the traditions to please the people.

A voice is heard in the crowd appealing to Cæsar. Cæsar hears and asks who calls. Casca, again acting as Cæsar's megaphone, commands silence. Cæsar says he hears a voice shriller than all the music crying to him above the confusion of the crowd. Later we shall find that Cæsar was deaf in one ear. Is there not, then, a keenness of perception here that the average person, using his five senses in the ordinary way, does not have? A Soothsayer is heard bidding Cæsar to beware the Ides of March. Cæsar asks the man's identity and Brutus speaks for the first time. He gives the information that it is a Soothsayer and repeats the warning. Granville Barker points out,[3] in commenting on this brief speech, that "its ominous weight is doubled in his mouth, its effect trebled by the innocent irony." Brutus, then, has heard all the man said, while Cæsar heard only a sound that was arresting, disturbing, discordant, and out of harmony with the occasion. Cæsar asks that the man be brought before him so that he may see his face. Cassius takes charge of the situation, calling the fellow to come out from the throng, and the man comes forth. The Soothsayer repeats the warning to Cæsar and Cæsar turns aside, dismissing him as a dreamer. Cæsar and his train, followed by the crowd, go out, and only Brutus and Cassius are left on the stage.

Cassius asks if Brutus is not going to watch the running of the races and Brutus' emphatic, "Not I" marks him immediately as one not interested in sports. Cassius pretends to urge him to go, though, as we shall soon find, he very much wishes to detain him. Brutus says he is not gamesome. Rather apologetically he explains that he is lacking in the "quick spirit", or liveliness, that is in Antony. However, he adds, he does not wish to hinder Cassius' enjoyment of the sport and so he will take his leave. Cassius

[3] In *Prefaces to Shakespeare.*

stops him with a direct verbal attack. He has noticed of late that Brutus' eyes have not shown the gentleness and love for him that he was accustomed to see in them. He accuses Brutus of putting a restraint on him, using a metaphor from horsemanship—curbing a friend who loves him, as he would a dumb animal. Brutus begs Cassius not to be deceived by any change in him. If he has concealed his feelings, he explains, his troubled countenance must be understood as being concerned only with himself. He has been vexed of late with conflicting emotions ("passions of some difference"), thoughts belonging exclusively to himself, which may have marred, or blemished, his behavior at different times. But he hopes that his good friends—among whom he counts Cassius—will not be grieved nor interpret his seeming neglect as meaning anything beyond the fact that poor Brutus is at war with himself and forgets to show his affection for his friends. The *New Clarendon Shakespeare* says, "Brutus calls himself 'poor' because he is distracted and miserable at the state of Rome."

Cassius replies that he has been mistaken and has misinterpreted the feelings that have moved Brutus, and because of his misunderstanding he has kept to himself thoughts of great value, worthy considerations. Suddenly he asks if Brutus can see his own face. Brutus' answer is "No," but the lines expressing his further observation are thought to have lost some words. Attention is called to the repetition of the preposition "by" as not being in Shakespeare's style. However, Brutus probably means to say that the eye discovers its own existence by its power of seeing other things. Cassius agrees that what Brutus has said is true (" 'T is just"), and continues to say that it is to be regretted that Brutus has no such similarly revealing mirrors that will discover his own worthiness so that he might behold his own image ("shadow"). He has heard, Cassius goes on, that many of the most respected men in Rome, except immortal Cæsar, in speaking of Brutus, and groaning under the yoke of the ages, have wished that the noble Brutus might have his eyes opened. Perhaps Brutus has caught a note of sarcasm in the word "immortal" as applied to Cæsar (Quiller-Couch says it was spoken with a sneer), and is on his guard immediately. He asks bluntly into what dangers Cassius is trying to lead him by suggesting that he seek in himself for qualities that are foreign to him. Gervinus says on this speech, "As the first hint, when Cassius initiates him into his ideas of a conspiracy, he feels that he is drawn into a foreign element. 'Into what dangers', he asks

> would you lead me, Cassius,
> That you would have me seek into myself
> For that which is not in me?'

His own inward voice calls him not to the deed."

Then, because of your confessed inadequacy, Cassius replies, be prepared to be enlightened. And, since you have admitted that you cannot see yourself except by reflection, I will be your glass and will modestly disclose to you a side of your own nature that you do not yet know. Brutus' facial expression evidently indicates doubt, and Cassius' next line means, Now don't be suspicious ("jealous") of me, gentle Brutus. If Cassius were a subject for merriment, or a common jester, he goes on, or the kind of person who meets every new protestation of friendship with the customary oaths that make such professions commonplace, or if he were the sort to fawn on men and take them to his heart, then afterwards speak slander of them, or if Brutus has ever known him at a banquet to make professions of friendship to all the disordered herd where ranks are not observed ("rout"), then Brutus may consider him dangerous. The subtleness of Cassius' approach stands out here because the things he mentions are the very things that are particularly distasteful to the studious Brutus—the mixing with the common herd, etc. The truth of Cassius' words about himself need not necessarily be questioned. His reasons for exclusiveness may not have been the same as those of Brutus, however.

A flourish and shout are heard coming from the games. Brutus says he fears the people are choosing Cæsar for their king. Cassius breaks in eagerly,

> "Ay, do you fear it?
> Then must I think you would not have it so."

Brutus admits that he does not wish to see Cæsar

made king, but adds that he, personally, loves him well. Then he breaks out in a mild protest at being detained by Cassius, asking why he holds him here so long, and demanding to know what it is he would impart to him. If honor and death must be looked upon together, he declares, he will look upon both of them impartially and with an untroubled mind, and the gods may speed his death if he does not love honor more than he fears death. Or, as the entire speech is interpreted in the *Furness Variorum,* "If the thing be for the public good, even though it cost me my very life, I will do it, for the cause of honour is more to me than the fear of death."

Cassius admits that he knows that one of the Roman "Virtues", honor, to be in Brutus as well as he knows his outward appearance. Well, he continues, honor is the subject of the story he is about to unfold. He does not know what Brutus and others think of this life, he reflects, but for himself he would as willingly cease to live as to be compelled to live in awe of another man like himself. More bluntly he goes on, I was born as free as Cæsar; so were you. We both have fed as well, and we can endure the winter's cold as well as he. He leaves his generalizing and tells of a specific time, a raw and gusty day when the Tiber River was dashing against her shores as if in anger, and Cæsar had challenged him to a swimming race with a certain point as an objective. Cassius plunged in without changing his clothes and called to Cæsar to follow. Cæsar joined him and they buffeted the roaring torrent with strong muscles,[4] throwing aside the water and making progress against it with contending spirits or keen rivalry. But before they could reach the goal they had set, Cæsar cried to Cassius to help him, admitting that otherwise he must sink. The historical Cæsar was an expert swimmer—a famous swimmer—and if this did occur it must have been a great humiliation to him. To continue with Cassius—he carried Cæsar from the Tiber on his back as Æneas, their ancestor, had carried his father, Anchises, from the flames of Troy. And this man, he continues vehemently, has now been made a god,[5] and Cassius has become a wretched creature who must bend his body if Cæsar gives him a careless nod of recognition. Cassius thinks of another personal story. It was when they were in Spain, probably during the last campaign, and Cæsar had a fever. When the chills came, Cassius noticed how Cæsar's body shook—yes, this god did shake and his lips lost their color. On the form of this sentence the *Arden Shakespeare* notes, "The natural form would be that the color fled from the lips. Cassius inverts it in order to suggest the idea of a coward deserting his colors." And the eye, Cassius goes on, lost its luster—the same eye whose glance ("bend") now awes the world. Cassius heard the sick man groan, yes, and that same tongue with which he bade the Romans write his

---

[4] "Sinews" in Shakespeare's time meant either muscles or nerves.

[5] The average reader misses something of the significance of this passage by not being familiar with the ancient custom of deifying rulers, described on page 46 of this study.

speeches in their books cried, "Give me some drink, Titinius," speaking to a friend of Cassius, and the voice was whining like that of a sick girl. Ye gods, the speaker exclaims, he is amazed that a man of such feeble self-command ("temper") should get the start —as in a race—of all the men in this majestic world and bear the palm of victory alone. The Arden edition of the play says, "The bearing of this speech is that Cæsar is a mere mortal, and very subject to the ills of the flesh; it develops the irony of 'immortal Cæsar' in line 60. Cassius is not arguing that Cæsar is an incompetent person, but that he is being treated as a deity when he is nothing of the kind, as his infirmity proves." But G. Wilson Knight says, "He does not, like Brutus, see two Cæsars; he sees only one—a frail, weak contemptible man." MacCallum finds "malicious contempt" in the accounts of the swimming match and the fever in Spain.

There comes the sound of another general demonstration from the crowd and Brutus says he fears these applauses are for some new honors that are being heaped upon Cæsar. Cassius, thus encouraged, pours out his thoughts in a diatribe against Cæsar. Why, man, he begins, with fiery passion for his subject, Cæsar bestrides the narrow world like a Colossus and we petty men walk under his huge legs and peep about with no hope but to find our graves, to which we must go without honor. The Colossus of Rhodes, which had been destroyed by an earthquake two hundred years before this time, had stood astride the entrance to the harbor at Rhodes. It was of such huge proportions that vessels passed in and out between its legs. Both Brutus and Cassius in their eastern travels must have seen the place where it once had stood. This seems to be our fate at the moment, Cassius' thought runs—this crawling about under the huge legs with no hope—but, he declares, there are times when men may become masters of their fate. The word "masters" is capitalized in the *First Folio,* indicating that it is to be emphasized. The fault of the present situation that finds us underlings is not in our stars but in ourselves, the speaker assures "dear Brutus." [6] Cassius is an Epicurean, and that philosophy denied supernatural intervention in, or control over, the affairs of men. Cassius now pronounces the names "Brutus" and "Cæsar", and asks what there might be in the name "Cæsar" and why that name should be proclaimed ("sounded") more than the name "Brutus". Write them together, he bids Brutus, and you will find that yours is as fair a name to look upon; pronounce them and the name "Brutus" is as becoming to the mouth; weigh them and "Brutus" is as heavy; conjure with them and the name of Brutus will stir the emotions of an audience [7] as readily as that of Cæsar. Is this true, or even logical? Commenting on this and kindred passages, Sir John Squire says, "[Shakespeare] can on

---

[6] Shakespeare seems, in a number of places, to express his disbelief in Astrology, which study was popular in his time.

[7] See "spirit"—O.E.D.

occasion convey whole characters and whole situations by the mere repetition, in various inevitable tones, of a single word . . . That iteration comes with tremendous effect in Cassius' speech made by all recalcitrants in all ages." He then quotes the speech we have just read, ending with "Brutus shall start a spirit as soon as Cæsar," and adds, "The truth is, though, that it wouldn't. O rhetorical idealism, how many crimes are committed in thy name!" Boas calls the speech "a singular piece of reasoning that Brutus and Cæsar must be in all points on a par because there is nothing to choose between their names as examples of the proper noun."

Another shout is heard. This stage direction is not in the *First Folio,* but has been interpolated here by modern editors as being the best place for the third shout described by Casca a little later in the scene (line 243). Each shout seems to act as a spur to Cassius' eloquence and he bursts out: Now in the name of all the gods at once, upon what meat does this our Cæsar feed that he has grown so great? He sees the age shamed by this one man's ascendency and declares that Rome has lost all her breed of noble blood. He asks when since the flood [8] there has been an age that was not famous for more than one great man. Until now, where could they, who talked of

[8] The story of Noah's flood could scarcely have been known to Cassius, but there were stories of such a flood in nearly every mythology. A note in the Bush edition of the play identifies this as "the flood, described by Ovid of which Deucalion and Pyrrha were the only survivors," and adds, "In the 16th and 17th centuries it was commonly identified with the story of Noah."

Rome, say that her wide walks [9] encompassed but one man. He makes a pun on the word "Rome," which in Shakespeare's time was pronounced more like "room", saying there's abundant room where there is only one man. He leaves the tirade against Cæsar and appeals to Brutus, reminding him, as he begins with an earnest or bitter "O", that he has heard their fathers speak of an earlier Roman Brutus who would have tolerated the eternal [10] devil himself as easily as he could have tolerated a king.

This reference to his ancestor, Lucius Junius,[11] who drove out the Tarquins, brings a reply from Brutus where the attack upon Cæsar has left him silent. That you love me, he begins, I have no doubt ("I am nothing 'jealous'" or suspicious). What you would work me to, or influence me to do, I have a conjecture or guess ("aim"). How much I have thought of all this and of the conditions of the times I will tell you later; but for the present I wish to be no further moved and so entreat you with my love to spare me. I will consider what you have said and whatever you may have to say in future I will bear with patience and will find an appropriate time both to hear and to answer such weighty or important

[9] "Walks" is the word in the *Folio*. It has been changed to "walls" by modern editors. Certainly walls seem to "encompass" better than walks, but the word "encompass" can mean "contain".

[10] Some critics, beginning with Johnson, prefer 'infernal" here. See discussion in *Furness Variorum*.

[11] On the matter of this relationship which is sometimes questioned, Plutarch says, "Some maintained that he was not of the house of Junius Brutus because of their malice and ill-will toward him after the death of Cæsar."

("high") things. Until then, my noble friend, reflect upon this: Brutus would rather be a villager than to think of ("repute") himself a son of Rome under the hard conditions that this time is likely to bring. To be a mere villager carried with it a certain stigma in the mind of a proud Roman. This speech is important. Does it show a man unwilling or unfit to meet the exigencies of the time? If unfit, does he regret his unfitness or take refuge in it?

Cassius says he is glad his weak words have struck even this much show of fire from Brutus. Has Brutus really shown any warm response to Cassius' arguments (if his observations may be called arguments) except a personal disturbance? Brutus, neither admitting nor disclaiming the "show of fire," observes that the games are over and Cæsar is returning. Cassius asks him to detain Casca by plucking at his coat as they pass, adding that Casca will tell them, in his sour fashion, whatever of importance has occurred at the games.

Cæsar and his train re-enter and Brutus calls his companion's attention to the angry glow on Cæsar's cheek, adding that all the rest of the train look as if they have been scolded. Calpurnia's cheek is pale, too, and Cicero's eyes have the fiery and ferret-like look that they have seen in the Capitol when he has been crossed in Senatorial debate. Cassius assures him that Casca will tell them all about it.

Cæsar calls Antony to him and begins speaking of Cassius. Editors do not indicate that this conversation is an aside, perhaps for the reason that it is obvious enough to be taken for granted. He would prefer to have men about him that are fat, Cæsar observes, sleek-headed men, such as sleep at night. Cassius has a lean and hungry look; he thinks too much. The word "thinks" as used here must have something of the sense of "broods." [12] Surely Cæsar does not object to a man who thinks things through from different viewpoints. However, we have also to consider "that certain Roman shyness" with regard to the effect of thinking upon action, mentioned before in this *Study*. Such brooding men, if we accept that reading, are dangerous, the speaker goes on. Antony replies in substance, Don't be afraid of him, Cæsar. He's not dangerous. Antony adds that Cassius is a noble Roman and well disposed. Cæsar insists that he would prefer to have him fatter, but adds that he has no fear of him. Yet if my name were compatible with fear, he continues, I do not know the man I should avoid so soon as that spare Cassius. MacCallum finds that "If he has not fears, he has at least misgivings in regard to Cassius, that come very much to the same thing. His anxiety is obvious." And Snider says, "How quickly he selects his real antagonist out of the multitude hanging around him." Cassius reads too much, Cæsar goes on, he is a great observer and looks quite through the deeds of men. Have we seen any evidence, so far, of Cassius' ability to look through the deeds of men? Has Cæsar anything to

[12] See O.E.D.

fear from Cassius' scrutiny of his own deeds? Is
Cæsar giving Cassius credit, undue credit, for an insight his reading ought to have brought him but may
have failed to do? Is it not possible that, at this time
when Rome was newly taking to reading, Cæsar
means to imply that Cassius reads too much of his
Epicurean philosophy into practical life? To some
people life is merely theory. Many things about life
must be learned by the laboratory method. Cæsar
himself had both the theoretical and the practical
knowledge of life. An Epicurean theorist, or any
other kind of theorist, would seem dangerous to him.
Cassius loves no plays as Antony does, the speaker
goes on; he hears no music. In *The Merchant of
Venice* Shakespeare has said,

> "The man that hath no music in himself
> Is fit for treasons, stratagems and spoils."

Cassius seldom smiles, Cæsar continues, and when
he does smile it seems as if he scorned his own nature,
or feelings, for permitting him to be moved to smile
at anything. Such men are never at ease while they
behold a greater person than themselves and therefore they are very dangerous. He explains to Antony
that he is merely speaking of what is to be feared and
not of what he really fears, ending with the words,
"for always I am Cæsar." This line must be examined later in a general discussion of Shakespeare's
presentation of the character of Cæsar, but for the
present we must consider some possible meanings.

Unquestionably, as most of the critics find, it sounds to us like boasting. But we must consider whether Cæsar, in his attempt to magnify the office he has so carefully built up, is not falling into the very human error of magnifying, or seeming to magnify, himself along with that office. The name "Cæsar" meant something. He had given it that meaning, and he may be here avowing his adherence to his ideal. Perhaps this was the language he had learned in Gaul for use in moments of crisis. He must have found the need of speaking some such language to his enemies, even to his own officers. And no one knew so well as he how much need there was in Rome for a fearless leadership. Then, too (another consideration), perhaps a man who had learned not to fear needed to speak of it more often in that still fear-ridden world. As they go out, Cæsar is asking Antony to tell him truly, or frankly, what he thinks of Cassius, requesting him to come to his right side since his left ear is deaf.

Casca has remained behind and now asks Brutus why he pulled him by the cloak, and Brutus bids him tell them what took place at the games that made Cæsar look so "sad." Most glossaries give the definitions "serious" or "sober" for the word "sad," but *The New Temple Shakespeare* says it has not quite the ordinary meaning of "sober" or "solemn," but means "put out or disgruntled." Casca seems, or pretends, to be under the impression that Brutus and Cassius were present at the games; but, when informed that they were not, he tells briefly how a crown was offered to Cæsar which he put by with the back of his hand—and Casca shows by gesture how it was done. He adds that then the people fell to shouting. By dint of questions Brutus gets the information that the crown was offered three times and refused three times—each time less decidedly than before. It requires a question from Cassius to elicit the information that it was Antony who offered the crown. The student must tread warily here and keep in mind that it is Casca and not Shakespeare who says that Cæsar put by the crown reluctantly. The historical scene is thus described by Froude: "Antony, his [Cæsar's] colleague in the consulship, approached with a tiara, and placed it on Cæsar's head saying, 'The people give you this by my hand.' That Antony had no sinister purpose is obvious. He perhaps spoke for the army; or it may be that Cæsar himself suggested Antony's action that he might end the agitation of such a dangerous subject. He answered in a loud voice 'that the Romans had no king but God' and ordered that the tiara should be taken to the Capitol and placed on the statue of Jupiter Olympus. The crowd burst into enthusiastic cheer; and an inscription on a brass tablet recorded that the Roman people had offered Cæsar a crown by the hands of the consul and that Cæsar had refused it."

If we accept this account of the scene given by the historian as the one Shakespeare believed, rather than the description he puts into the mouth of Casca, it may seem necessary to account for the "sad" look on Cæsar's face, also for the paleness of his wife and the disturbance of Cicero. The interpretation of the word "sad", as given above, conforms to the story as given by Casca, but the other meaning is a little more in keeping with the story as given by the historian. A number of things might have made Cæsar sad, above all the thought that only a few, if any, could understand his high motives in refusing the crown. Calpurnia's paleness may be attributed to the strain of the day's events and the seriousness of her husband's situation. As for Cicero and his agitation, the entire scene would be distasteful to him—his boyhood playmate offered a crown and by the illiterate, unpolished Antony who was disgracing the sacred consulship by running in the games, like the common person he was—the consulship he himself had graced and glorified so impressively. The Senate at its very worst had never offered him a greater insult! These very natural reactions to the off-stage scene have been seized upon by Brutus as an explanation for something that may not actually have taken place.

Brutus urges Casca to tell the manner of the offer and the refusal, and Casca declares he could as easily be hanged as tell the details. It was mere foolery anyway, and he paid no attention. Would details be wanting or be evaded in a more serious, more authentic account? Casca did see, he continues, that Mark

Antony offered Cæsar a crown—not a crown neither, but a coronet, and Cæsar refused it. To Casca's thinking it seemed that Cæsar was very loath to take his fingers off it; and, when he refused it for the third time, the rabble hooted and clapped their toil-worn hands and threw up their sweaty night-caps [13] and sent forth such a quantity of stinking breath that it almost choked Cæsar and he fell down. Casca himself dared not laugh for fear of breathing the bad air. The story of Cæsar's falling strikes a responsive chord in the mind of Cassius. It is along the line his thought has been pursuing—the physical weakness of Cæsar. Shakespeare suggests his craftiness and desire for more such information in the eager, invidious, "But soft, I pray you; did Cæsar swound?" Casca, nothing daunted, adds details and Brutus admits that Cæsar has the "falling-sickness"—which we know as epilepsy. Cassius embraces the opportunity to put in the argument that it is not Cæsar who has the falling-sickness but Brutus, himself, and "honest Casca". Casca pretends not to grasp Cassius' meaning, or perhaps misses the point, but reiterates what he has said, adding that he is no true man if the people did not alternately applaud and hiss Cæsar, as they do the players in the theatre.

[13] "Shakespeare's allusion to night-caps in Julius Cæsar has never been supported by evidence that this kind of head-covering was worn by the Romans." (*Costume in Elizabethan Drama*—Linthecum.) The day caps of Elizabethans were greasy because they kept them on at meals (to prevent lice falling into the food) and ate with their fingers from trenchers. Shakespeare's sensitiveness found some of these things revolting—and he has been accused of hating the common people.

Casca has given an unpleasant picture of Cæsar that seems inconsistent with the character as we have been able to build it so far. If it were not for the agreement of Brutus in the matter of the falling-sickness, we should be able to pass by the account with little comment, as part of Casca's exaggeration. Such facts on the subject as are available are these: Shakespeare took the story of Cæsar's falling-sickness from Plutarch, who, according to Baring-Gould and others, went to Cæsar's enemies for much of his material. There is an oft-repeated story that in his youth Cæsar sometimes extricated himself from a difficult situation by feigning falling-sickness. It was an age when such mountebank actions would not be frowned upon as they would be to-day. Surely the mature Cæsar had put away such buffoonery, but he could not live down the earlier impression he had made. Such light as modern study turns on the causes of epilepsy seem to belie the possibility of any such disaffection in a man of Cæsar's perfect physical, mental, and moral health. It is not unlikely that the unfortunate youthful trick was used later to interpret the normal slowing-down of mental processes, or any brief, temporary loss of memory common to aging persons. Whether Shakespeare believed that Cæsar had falling-sickness we do not know. Possibly the thought would not have been so unpleasant to him as it is to us. It was a story that was told, and is still told. Shakespeare puts it into the mouth of the envious, disloyal Casca, and permits the truthful Brutus to agree—and we may take it or leave it.[14]

Brutus inquires what Cæsar said when he came to himself and Casca continues, embellishing the tale with a ready, but, we suspect, none too scrupulous tongue. Cæsar had opened his doublet [15] and offered his throat to be cut, the speaker says, declaring that, if he, Casca, had been a working man, or a man of any of the trades ("occupation") he would have taken Cæsar at his word. He emphasizes the declaration by saying that, if this was not his reaction, he hopes he may go to hell among the rogues. And so Cæsar fell, the speaker goes on, knowing that he has one eager and one interested listener. When Cæsar came to himself, he desired the people to know that it was due to his infirmity if he had said or done anything amiss.[16] Three or four wenches had cried, "Alas, good soul" and forgave him with all their hearts, but Casca considers them not worth heeding since they would have done the same if Cæsar had stabbed their mothers.

[14] See discussion of the subject in *The Furness Variorum.*

[15] The doublet was a garment of Shakespeare's time.

[16] Shakespeare found in his Plutarch the story of Cæsar's opening his doublet to his friends after "they went unto him in the market place . . . to tell him what honors they had decreed for him in his absence. But he . . . answered them that his honors had more need to be cut off than enlarged." Cæsar's explanation, attributing his action (opening his doublet) to falling-sickness, follows. All this smacks of the youthful buffoonery, which Plutarch accepted. Shakespeare may have acknowledged it as one of the tales that were told about Cæsar and put it into the mouth of Casca, whose untruthfulness would seem obvious to his audience. We need not accept it as truth.

Cassius asks if Cicero said anything. Casca answers that he spoke Greek, that those who understood him smiled at one another and shook their heads. It was all Greek to Casca. This may not mean literally that Casca does not understand Greek. It is quite likely a gibe at the growing acceptance of Greek thought and may express Casca's own preference for Roman ways. A note in the *Arden Shakespeare,* discussing Cicero, says "Shakespeare's dramatic scheme allows him no place in determining the course of events, with the curious result that the greatest of Roman orators is introduced into the tragedy to speak eight and a half unimportant lines." However, do we not find here, as we may later, that the Cicero of the play is a man whose opinion counted? The historical Cicero was also a man whose opinion counted, although he did little to change the course of events. A writer quoted in the *Furness Variorum* says, "The answer, 'He spoke Greek,' gives us the complete character of Cicero. . . . He has not sufficient force of character to decide definitely . . . and he does not wish to express a decided opinion easily comprehensible in order that he may always be free . . . it is not for him to speak now with the common people, nor should so eccentric a character as Casca understand him. . . . If Shakespeare could have read and studied all Cicero's collected writings in the original, never, in my opinion, would there have offered itself a phrase more characteristic than, 'He spoke Greek.' "

Casca then voluntarily gives the information that Marullus and Flavius have been punished for pulling the scarfs off the statues of Cæsar. There was no scarf in the Roman dress. It belongs to the age of chivalry. It was made of silk and drawn across one shoulder and down to the waist-line on the other side. It was originally used for carrying small articles. Later it became merely decorative. Shakespeare would not hesitate to drape the statue of Cæsar with one of these scarfs familiar to his own time. However, some of the critics identify these scarfs as garlands. Casca bids farewell to the other two and adds that there was more "foolery" if he could remember it. The word "foolery" to some extent describes his attitude toward the proceedings he had seen fit to attend. It should be noted that Casca made himself quite prominent, and seemed deferential to Cæsar, in getting the attention of the rabble to what Cæsar was saying, but that in the presence of Cassius he lets his tongue go unguardedly.

Cassius invites Casca to have supper with him and, on finding that he has a previous engagement, or says he has, asks him to dine with him to-morrow. Casca's reply seems rude to us—at least unnecessarily frank. Cassius promises a good dinner. This, according to accounts of the times, would probably include an ample array of hors-d'œuvre, consisting of many varieties of lettuce, artichokes, olives, leeks, mallows, asparagus, and cucumbers. After these would come mushrooms, snails, oysters, fresh or cooked, sardines and other fish, salted or in oil. Then would come other courses including game and fish of every sort, sauces and condiments without end. The sweets, or dessert course, would consist of fruits, both fresh and preserved, and cakes. Wine would be served throughout the dinner, probably cooled in snow. The meal would begin with a prayer to the gods.[17]

When Casca goes out Brutus remarks on what a blunt fellow he has become, adding that he was "quick mettle", or of high spirits and keen ability, when he went to school. So we find Casca a man who has not fulfilled the promise of his youth. Mac-Callum remarks that such promising youngsters when they fail "often do so from certain lack of moral fibre." The psychiatrist could tell us a great deal more about them, but it is sufficient for our purposes to know that, having failed themselves, they are often extremely envious of others who succeed. The clever Cassius will select Casca for a key position. Now he is saying to Brutus that Casca still has spirit in the execution of any bold or noble enterprise, no matter how much he may put on the appearance of slug-gishness or disinterestedness. One wonders, in exam-ining this sentence, whether Cassius did not bethink himself quickly after using the word "bold" and add the word "noble" especially for the ears of Brutus. He apologizes for Casca's rudeness, comparing it to a sauce which he adds to his wit, or wisdom, to make

[17] See *The Roman's World*—Moore.

what he says more digestible, or acceptable. Brutus agrees and starts to take his leave, saying that if Cassius wishes to speak with him, he will come to him, or, if Cassius prefers, he may come to Brutus' house and Brutus will be expecting him. Cassius seems to agree to the latter plan and requests Brutus to be thinking of the affairs of the world in the meantime. Do we not much prefer that Cassius should go to Brutus for this conference, than that Brutus should go to Cassius?

Left alone, Cassius soliloquizes, speaking in imagination to Brutus. Brutus is noble, he observes, but adds, perhaps a little gloatingly, that he can see how easily that honorable metal can be worked upon and its intrinsic character changed. Therefore it is better that noble minds keep with other noble minds. This is an admission that his own mind is not noble or, perhaps a little more accurately, that he recognizes that his intentions are not noble. For who, he asks, is so firm that he cannot be swayed or won from his fixed ideals? Cæsar dislikes me ("bears me hard"), he goes on, but he loves Brutus. The next sentence presents a difficulty in that it is not clear whether the pronoun "he" (at the beginning of line 319) refers to Cæsar or to Brutus. The edition edited by Douglass Bush gives the alternative meanings as follows: "If I, Cassius, were Brutus, and Brutus were Cassius then (1) Cæsar would not cajole me as easily as he now does Brutus; or, (2) Brutus should not win me from loyalty to Cæsar so easily as I am winning him.

Perhaps (2) is preferable." Now Cassius declares his plan of throwing into Brutus' windows papers on which will be written messages, purportedly from citizens, on the subject of the high opinion Rome has of him, Brutus. Also there will be obscure hints in these writings on the subject of Cæsar's ambition. Cassius seems confident that these papers will accomplish his purpose, for he concludes by saying that once these messages are delivered into the hands of Brutus, Cæsar should make himself secure, for with Brutus' help they will unseat him or worse days will come.

This is Cassius' first soliloquy. First soliloquies of important characters are of great significance in Shakespeare. Often we are given a glimpse into the very heart of the character in a few lines. However, they are not always truthful self-revelations, but may describe a temporary state of mind. MacCallum finds this speech perplexing and suggests that, "Probably Cassius is making the worst of his own case, and is indulging that vein of self-mockery and scorn that Cæsar observed in him" (line 206, this scene). This author mentions that at first sight the soliloquy "seems to place Cassius in the ranks of Shakespeare's villains along with his Iagos and Richards rather than with the mixed characters, compact with good and evil, with whom, nevertheless, we feel that he is akin." With this warning against a too hasty labelling of Cassius as a villain, the student will be prepared to consider this same critic's suggestion that, in spite of the taint of enviousness and spite, "Cassius is far from being a despicable or even an unattractive character" and Chamber's statement that "Cassius is not without sparks of greatness in him."

In considering the character of Cassius, two pairs of words must be studied discriminatingly. We must first differentiate between "jealousy" and "envy." An adequate, one might almost say the best, distinction is to be found in the maxim, "Jealousy in a way is right and reasonable, for it defends what is ours, or what we think is ours; but envy cannot endure the happiness of others." [18] The question one must ask about Cassius, then, is: Was he defending himself or anything that was rightfully his or his country's against Cæsar? The other two words to be studied are "opposition" and "prejudice." One may be decidedly opposed to someone or something without necessarily being prejudiced. One may have what are to him good and sufficient reasons for his objections and, even if his reasons do not seem sound to others, they are honest reasons if they seem sound to him. A prejudice is a stubborn stand that is taken and held against all reason, a refusal to consider any view but the one already accepted. Is Cassius opposed to Cæsar for good reasons of his own, even though they may be unsound reasons? Or, has he taken a stand that he is holding against all reason? Are the objections he has named based on standards of nobility, or are they all petty fault-finding? How much do they

[18] La Rochefoucauld (1613–1680).

have to do with Cæsar's accomplishments and his aims? To what extent are they merely a catalogue of physical weaknesses that may have little or nothing to do with a man's character or his fitness for office? Has Brutus the kind of reasoning power and experience to meet these objections or prejudices? A word of caution is needed here. No matter how much of personal feeling we may find, whether it be jealousy, envy, or something else, one important thing to note in the speeches of Cassius is his strong opposition to the rule of one man. In this he expresses the typical and traditional Roman attitude almost as much as Brutus. Shakespeare makes no mention of the prætorships bestowed upon Brutus and Cassius. There were sixteen of these prætors, or magistrates, and the highest rank among them was given to Brutus though that first place belonged to Cassius by virtue of his seniority and his military record. Shakespeare's omission of this historical material seems to indicate his belief that it was not to any great extent this preferment that was influencing Cassius against Cæsar. If that were rankling particularly, some jealousy would be aroused against Brutus. However, we have Cassius' statement that Cæsar dislikes him, with no proofs given.

We shall need to watch in studying the character of Cassius to see how much his Epicurean philosophy influences his decisions and actions. A smattering of philosophy may do more harm than good. Misapplied, it may even destroy all human sympathy.

Cæsar may have had some such thought in mind in mentioning Cassius' reading. Epicureanism has been called a "refuge philosophy". It taught that man has "nothing to fear—either from the gods who live in careless bliss, remote from the world and unconcerned to punish or reward us, or from the life to come, since our souls are as mortal as our bodies and Death is but a sleep that has no waking." [19] This was a welcome belief to the many who "were in bondage to the fear of death or to that mental disquietude which is produced sooner or later by polytheism." [20] The Epicurean held also that "pleasure (or absence of pain) is the only good known to the senses; and that the best pleasure, as being accompanied by no painful want, is a perfect harmony of body and mind to be sought in plain living and in virtue." [21] "The modern English sense of the word 'Epicurean', i.e., 'devoted to refined and tasteful sensuous enjoyment' (O.E.D.) misrepresents the teaching of Epicurus." [22]

The Stoic, unlike the Epicurean, believed in the providential government of the world. *The Cambridge Ancient History* finds in their teachings "an intolerance of imperfection amounting to a sense of 'sin', an uncompromising idealism and a demand for resignation before the All-Supreme—which we associate with the Semitic spirit and find later in Islam,

[19] *The Cambridge Ancient History.*
[20] *Ibid.*
[21] *Oxford Companion to Classical Literature.*
[22] *Ibid.*

but which were new to the thought of Hellas." Their founder (Zeno) introduced the words *"Duty"* and *"Conscience"*. The work just quoted continues, "Their creed has often been lauded as the noblest embodiment of pre-Christian thought, but it is at best a gospel of Detachment (and as such can be paralleled in Indian ethics), far removed from the gospel of Love." The Stoic had an unconquerable soul. Brutus had a strong leaning toward Stoicism, though he was known as a Platonist.

The Greek philosophies, it must be remembered, were as engrafted branches on the life and thought of Rome, where developments, conditions, and temperament differed widely from the Greek. In a sense the Roman was not to the philosophic manner born, his chief concern being with practical everyday living. Perhaps, as the play develops, we shall glimpse Shakespeare's thought of what the philosophies of the several characters meant to them in a world that was "sick with a moral plague." [23]

[23] Froude.

ACT I—SCENE III

IT IS late evening of the fourteenth of March, a stormy evening. The scene is a street in Rome, very likely near the house of Julius Cæsar. Casca enters with drawn sword and is met by Cicero, who inquires if he has escorted Cæsar home. Before Casca answers, Cicero notices that he is agitated and inquires why he is out of breath, why he stares so. Casca asks if the other is not perturbed by the storm, by the fact that the settled order of the earth [1] is shaken like an infirm thing. On this line the *Furness Variorum* finds that "it needs not be interpreted as an actual earthquake. . . . It means only that the agitations in the heavens were so violent that they seemed even to portend that the earth itself would fall back into its original chaos." Then Casca bursts out, exclaiming that he has seen many tempests on land and sea, when angry winds have split the knotty oak trees, and when the ocean swelled and raged as if its foamy waves were ambitious to reach the exalted elevation of the threatening clouds; but never until to-night did he go through a tempest that dropped fire. He offers two theories; either there is civil strife in heaven, or else the people of the earth,

[1] See "sway," *Onions' Glossary.*

who are too impertinent or presumptuous [2] with the gods, have angered them into destroying the earth. Cicero, still composed in spite of Casca's panic, asks if he has seen anything more wonderful than what has been related. Professor Kittredge finds that "Dreadful as it is, the tempest does not seem to Cicero enough to account for Casca's panic." Casca gives more details. A common slave, a familiar figure in the streets of Rome, held up his left hand and it was illuminated by a fire twenty times the strength of a torch, and yet the hand was not sensitive to the fire and remain unscorched. Besides, Casca goes on, he met a lion near the Capitol and has not put up his sword since the encounter.[3] The lion glared or "glazed" at him and went morosely by without annoying him. "Glazed" is the word in the First Folio. It meant "stare", perhaps with glassy eyes, and is still in use in that sense in parts of rural England. Casca continues his story, telling of a group of a hundred women huddled together, ghastly looking, terrified women, who swore they had seen men all in fire walking up and down the streets. And yesterday, he adds, an owl sat in the market-place at noon, hooting and shrieking. When all these omens or portents

[2] *Onions' Glossary* says the word "saucy" was in Shakespeare's time "an epithet of more serious condemnation than at present."

[3] "We do not know that lions were kept in the *Capitol,* but they were kept in the Tower of London, which may well have represented the Capitol to Shakespeare and his audience. In Act II, Sc. 1, 3, the Capitol is pointed to as due east and this was the position of the Tower from the Globe Theatre in Bankside."

The New Clarendon Shakespeare

occur at once, he warns, let not man attempt to give reasons or explain that they are natural happenings. He firmly believes, Casca asserts, that they are portentous or ominous warnings to the country ("climate") in which they occur.[4] Cicero agrees that, indeed, it is a strangely ordered time, but adds that men are inclined to construe, or interpret, things after their own fashion, which is often at variance with the meaning of the things themselves. Casually he inquires if Cæsar intends to come to the Senate to-morrow, and Casca answers that Cæsar instructed Antony to send word to Cicero that he would be present. It should be noticed here that Cæsar considered Cicero important enough to be informed of his intention. Cicero bids Casca good night, more interested, apparently, in to-morrow's session of the Senate than in the storm, but giving as an excuse for leaving the disturbed sky, which makes walking about unpleasant. Cicero goes on his way, the scholarly man undisturbed by the alarm of the superstitious, unstable Casca. We shall learn very soon that Cassius had not broached the subject of the conspiracy at the dinner to which he invited Casca a month ago. Casca may still be supposed to know nothing definite of the plot. Is it the storm alone, then, that has so greatly agitated him, or does some of the disturbance come from uncertain speculations and whispered rumors?

Cassius enters and the recognition is by voice only,

[4] A similar passage in found in *Hamlet,* I, I, 113–125.

so dark is the night. These men would not be wearing their white togas in the rain. For bad weather and for travelling, the Romans wore, as an outer garment, a cape made of heavy material, sometimes felt, sometimes leather. The togas were whitened by the fuller with pipe clay, and required a great deal of attention. Casca exclaims about the stormy night, but Cassius replies that it is a very pleasing night to honest men, seeming to ignore the reference to the storm. Casca asks whoever knew the heavens to be so threatening, and Cassius answers that they who have recognized the great faults that fill the earth know that the menace of heaven must be pending. For his own part he has walked about the streets submitting his body to the elements, his cape flung back, his tunic opened, or slipped down,[5] so that his bosom is bared to the thunder-stone, a stone fabulously supposed to be discharged by thunder. Even when the zig-zag, blue lightning seemed like a rent or opening in the very breast of heaven, he had stood boldly exposed in the place where it might strike. Casca asks why he tempted the heavens, declaring that it is the part of men to fear and tremble when, by these signs ("tokens"), the most mighty of the gods send such heralds to astonish mankind. One is tempted to change the word "by" in this sentence to "as" and to read "as tokens." A "token" in Shakespeare's time was a "plague spot," a boil under

---

[5] Shakespeare confuses the Roman tunic with the doublet of his own time which could be unbuttoned.

the arm which was the first and unmistakable symptom of the plague. Also, the word "token" has the sense of "something given as a symbol and evidence of a right or privilege, upon the presentation of which the right or privilege may be exercised." [6] Either of these definitions would give additional strength to the sentence, and would emphasize Casca's superstition, the one being identified with the Elizabethan fear of the plague and the other, perhaps, with primitive fear of the elements. In this second case Casca would seem to be saying that the thunder and lightning are the gods' symbol of their right and privilege to send further punishment upon the world.

Cassius tells Casca he is dull and either lacks the mental alertness that should be in every Roman or he does not use those "sparks of life"; he looks pale and stands gazing; he "puts on" fear and "casts" himself in wonder to see the strange turmoil ("impatience") of the heavens. Cassius is here suggesting that Casca deliberately permits himself to fear and wonder, or throws himself into this state. Then Cassius explains what seem to him to be the true reasons for the things that have taken place—the presence of fires and gliding ghosts, the change of birds and beasts from their disposition and nature, and the unusual speculation, or prognostication, even of old men, fools, and children. The passage as it stands in the text is obscure, the chief structural difficulty being with the word "calculate." *The New Temple*

[6] O.E.D.

Shakespeare says, "The real trouble is that we do not want a verb till we arrive at *change* in the next line, that therefore *calculate* should be an adjective, and that there is no satisfactory sense for it." Cassius goes on with his argument, saying that, if Casca will consider the true cause why all these things change from the common usage ("ordinance"),[7] their own natures and functions ("performed faculties") to this unnatural behavior ("monstrous quality"), he will find that heaven has endowed ("infused") them with new qualities ("spirits") in order to make them instruments of fear and warning concerning some monstrous state of affairs. Then he comes out boldly and says he could name a man who is much like this dreadful night, a man who thunders, opens graves, and roars like the lion in the Capitol, and this man is no mightier than Casca or himself in physical capacity ("personal action") yet has grown as prodigious and threatening as these strange eruptions in nature. Casca catches his meaning immediately and names Cæsar. Cassius will not admit the identity of the man as yet, but goes on to say that Romans still have their physical inheritance from their ancestors; but it is to be woefully regretted that they no longer have their fathers' minds, but are governed by their mothers' milder spirits or dispositions. The fact that they are so patient in enduring their yoke shows that they are womanish. Casca, speaking more directly than Cassius has done, says he has heard that the

[7] *Onions' Glossary.*

senators mean to establish Cæsar as king to-morrow, that he is to wear his crown by sea and land in every country except Italy.

The mention of the crown stirs all Cassius' deepest feeling and he declares his own attitude toward such an eventuality. He knows where he will wear his dagger (in his heart) and he will thus deliver himself from bondage. He glories in the fact that the gods thus enable weak men to be strong enough to take their own lives and, by this assistance, help to defeat the tyrants. No stony tower, he declares, nor walls of beaten brass, nor airless dungeon can imprison a strong spirit; but life, being weary of its worldly bars, or hindrances, never lacks the power to free itself. And since he knows this himself, he concludes, all the world may know that such part of tyranny as he is called upon to bear can be shaken off at his own pleasure. On this speech *The Arden Shakespeare* notes that, "if a little bombastic, this speech has the ring of genuine feeling in it. Cassius is not merely stirred by envy. . . . In the very next speech it is envy that predominates again." Boas quotes the passage as "a cry of melancholy grandeur." MacCallum says, "He may play the devil's advocate in regard to individuals, but he is capable of high enthusiasm for his cause, such as it is. We must share his calenture of excitement as he strides about the streets in the tempest that fills Casca with superstitious dread and Cicero with discomfort at the nasty weather. His republicanism may be a nar-

row creed, but at least he is willing to be a martyr
to it; when he hears that Cæsar is to wear a crown,
his resolution is prompt and Roman-like:

> I know where I will wear my dagger then;
> Cassius from bondage will deliver Cassius."

Casca says he, too, can take his own life by the
sword and adds his own echo of Cassius' thought that
every man in bondage bears in his own hand the
power to end his captivity as one may cancel any
other kind of bond—by death. Cassius then dilates
on the subject of Cæsar's tyranny, real or otherwise,
asking first why it is permitted. He pretends to pity
poor Cæsar because of the position in which he finds
himself. Cæsar would not be a wolf but that he sees
that the Romans are as docile as sheep; he would not
be a lion if Romans were not as meek as the female
deer. Cassius thus "sees in Cæsar's ascendency nothing but a proof of the degeneracy of the times." [8]
Hudson's explanation of the next lines is, "The idea
seems to be that as men start a huge fire with worthless straws or shavings, so Cæsar is using the degen-
erate Romans of the time to set the whole world
ablaze with his own glory." This writer comments
further: "Cassius' enthusiastic hatred of the 'mighti-
est Julius' is irresistibly delightful. For a good hater
is the next best thing to a true friend; and Cassius'
honest gushing malice is far better than Brutus' stab-

[8] Boas.

bing sentimentalism." It is not, indeed, "irresistibly delightful" to see one so wrought up by his own feelings that he can find Julius Cæsar a "vile thing"? Cassius now speaks to his own grief, asking where it has led him. Perhaps, he says to Casca, he is speaking to one who is a willing bondman. If so, he will be publicly called to account and must answer for his seditious words. He declares that dangers are a matter of indifference. In his excitement he has ignored Casca's acquiescence a few lines back. Casca assures him that he is speaking to Casca, a man who is no mocking ("fleering") tell-tale. He offers his hand as a pledge of faith and says, If you will be active ("factious"), or begin action, for the redress of all these griefs, I will go as far as the one who goes farthest, or as we should say, as far as anyone.

The bargain is made, and sealed by a handclasp, then Cassius tells of the definite plans. He has influenced certain noble-minded Romans to undertake with him an enterprise involving honor, but with possible danger in the consequences. He knows that these men are waiting for him by this time in Pompey's porch. Pompey's superb theatre, the first to be built of stone, had been erected on his return from the East, out of the vast wealth he had brought with him—to ingratiate himself with the people, it has been said. It accommodated an audience of 17,000. There was a colonnaded porch designed to provide shelter for passers-by in inclement weather. One of the great halls was called the "Curia Pompeia" and contained a magnificent statue of Pompey. It was in this hall that the Senate was to meet on the morrow, because the Curia in the Forum was being rebuilt.

Cassius goes on, saying that now on this fearful night there is no stir and no walking in the streets, and the complexion or color of the sky ("element") is in appearance ("favour") like the work they have in hand, bloody, fiery, and most terrible. Casca hears someone coming and warns Cassius to stand close, or hidden in the shadows, but Cassius recognizes Cinna by his walk and inquires where he is going in such haste. Cinna answers that he was trying to find Cassius. Then he asks if the other is Metellus Cimber, and is told that it is Casca who is included in ("incorporate to") their enterprise. Cassius asks if the others are waiting for him, but Cinna replies to the first part of Cassius' speech and says he is glad Casca has joined them. He then goes on to speak of the fearful night, adding that two or three of "us," evidently the conspirators, have seen strange sights. Cassius is not interested in the sights, but asks again if the conspirators are waiting for him. Cinna answers that they are, then bursts out with the wish that they might win the noble Brutus to their party. Before he has finished, Cassius bids him be content. He gives him a paper which is to be laid in the prætor's chair. Cinna is to throw another paper, which Cassius now gives him, into Brutus' window. A third paper, or placard, is to be set up with sealing wax upon the statue of Junius Brutus.[9] According to Plutarch, "under the image of his ancestor Junius Brutus—they wrote: O, that it pleased the gods thou wert now alive, Brutus." When these things are done, Cinna is to go to Pompey's porch where he will find Cassius and Casca. Cassius then inquires whether Decius Brutus and Trebonius are there, making sure of two who were close to Cæsar, and Cinna answers that all are present except Metellus Cimber, who has gone to find Cassius at his house. It will be recalled that Cinna took Casca for Metellus. These touches suggest that they knew only a few people were abroad. Cinna says he will hurry along and bestow the papers as Cassius has directed him, and he goes out. Cornelius Cinna, father of this man, had, on the death of Marius, become the leader of the popular party. He had been absolute master of Rome. His daughter was Cæsar's first wife. The son, Cæsar's former brother-in-law, now seems willing to be a kind of errand-boy for the conspirators. As he goes out Cassius instructs him for the second time to repair to Pompey's porch when he has finished the task.

Turning to Casca, Cassius says that before day-

---

[9] Shakespeare shows Cassius disposing of these papers at this time, though it must have been done much earlier. It was too late, now, for Brutus to find the scroll in the prætor's chair or the placard, before the meeting of the Senate. This is only another example of what Horatio Bridges calls Shakespeare's "divine carelessness" that sets him apart from Francis Bacon, whose scholarly, scientific mind was "so obsessed by the necessity of removing every inconsistency" that he was incapable of Shakespeare's "superb indifference".

light, after the meeting, they will go to see Brutus at his house. He gives the information, withheld from Cinna, that three-fourths of Brutus are already won over to their cause and the entire man will yield at this interview. Was Brutus so far won over when we last saw him with Cassius? Do we not feel certain that Cassius has paid that visit that was arranged as they parted on the day of the Lupercal? Why would Shakespeare choose to draw a veil over that meeting? Casca exclaims that Brutus stands high in the love of the people and that that which would appear offense in Cassius or himself would be changed to virtue and to worthiness by the alchemy of his approving countenance. Alchemy, it will be recalled, attempted to transmute base metals into precious ones. We may note here, with the *New Clarendon* editors, that "Casca, in spite of his cynical depreciation of others, bears unqualified testimony to Brutus". Cassius replies to Casca's remark that he has right well described or understood ("conceited") the worth of Brutus and the conspirators' great need of him. He urges that they go now, since it is after midnight, adding that before daylight they will awaken Brutus and make sure of him.

Commenting briefly on the three principal characters in this scene, the editors of the *Arden Shakespeare* say, "Cicero is sententious and wears an air of philosophic calm. He was indeed prouder of his philosophy than of his oratory . . . Casca, as always, allows the moment's mood to control him, and the mood itself is controlled by the immediate circumstances. Both are in strong contrast to Cassius, to whom the conditions of the moment are of interest just so far as he sees his way to making use of them for the ends he holds steadily and unceasingly in view."

Cicero has disappeared in the darkness and, although he was accounted the second man in Rome, he will not appear again in the play. The historical Cicero had been on the side of Pompey in the war, but had been forgiven by Cæsar. The Senate, having failed to defeat Cæsar in the field, had smothered him with honors, and Cicero became their mouthpiece. Cicero always wavered and always thought first of his own safety. He made a great speech in the Senate a few weeks before the assassination, lauding Cæsar to the skies. A few sentences will give the flavor of the speech: [10] "How can we praise, how can we love you sufficiently? By the gods, the very walls of this house are eloquent with gratitude. . . . We live by your goodness. The sword is now sheathed. Those whom we have lost fell in the fury of the fight, not one by the resentment of the conqueror. Cæsar, if he could, would bring back to life many who are dead. . . . The ages that are to be will try you with minds, it may be, less prejudiced than ours, uninfluenced either by desire to please you or by envy of your greatness. . . . From my own heart I say, and

---

[10] Portions of the speech may be found conveniently in Froude's biography.

I speak for others as well as myself, we will stand as sentries over your safety, and we will interpose our own bodies between you and any danger which may menace you." [11] In this speech he referred to Cæsar and his deeds as "immortal". One wonders how much the speech had to do with infuriating Cassius.

After the assassination Cicero said, "What difference is there between advice beforehand and approbation afterwards? What does it matter that I wished it to be done, or rejoiced that it was done? Is there a man, save Antony and those who were glad to have Cæsar reign over us, that did not wish him to be killed? All were at fault, for all the *Boni* joined in killing him, so far as lay in them. Some were not consulted, some wanted courage, some opportunity. All were willing." [12]

[11] Froude.
[12] *Ibid.*

It is said that Cicero grew up in a fuller's establishment, and one is tempted to make a quip about his later whitewashing of people and events.

ACT II—SCENE I

WHILE the conspirators are having their meeting, Brutus has not slept well. About two o'clock he has gotten up, put on his night-robe, and gone out into his garden, or orchard. This colonnaded garden is probably extensive in proportion to a large, rambling house, and would have a fountain, as well as flower-beds and shrubbery. Brutus calls to Lucius, his personal attendant, and while he waits remarks that he cannot tell by the progress of the stars how near it is to day. The storm has evidently abated but the stars are not out. He calls Lucius a second time and envies him his sound sleep. With a touch of impatience he asks when the boy is coming, and calls his name more commandingly. Lucius enters, asking if his lord called. Brutus tells him to go and light a taper or candle in his study and then come and call him. A flint would have to be struck to light this taper.

If we were able to follow Lucius into the study and linger awhile after the taper is lighted, we should find "book-cases about six feet high, closed by solid doors, each case fitting its own niche in the wall. . . . The cases . . . no doubt of valuable woods, [were] possibly adorned with ivory and numbered. On opening the doors of the case we should see each shelf supporting its own pile of libri, papyrus rolls, stacked like fire-wood, one end of the roll facing outward, displaying its attached tag (*titulus*). This was a parchment label bearing the name of the author and his work." [1] Here and there in the room would be busts in bronze or marble of the master's favorite authors.

Left alone, Brutus speaks directly of the conspiracy. If one were reading the play for the first time, he would doubtless feel a shock at the frank statement, "It must be by his death," since Cassius has said he was only three-fourths won over. Just how much Cassius has had to do in winning him thus far, we do not know, since Brutus declared his intention of thinking the thing through himself; but we may rest assured Cassius has not hesitated to use all his persuasive powers. For his own part, Brutus goes on, he has no personal cause to spurn Cæsar, but there are general, public reasons. He begins to weigh these reasons. Cæsar wishes to be crowned, but what would be the result? There is the question of how it might change his nature. It should be noticed that Brutus thinks there must be a change in Cæsar before he becomes dangerous. It is a bright day that brings forth the adder from his hiding-place, the speaker observes. Applied to the situation he is considering, the comparison would seem to infer that at present the prospects in Rome are bright. The fact of some dangerous thing emerging on the scene asks

[1] *The Roman's World*—Moore.

or requires ("craves") wary walking, his thought continues. If we crown him then, he grants, we give him a dangerous weapon like the sting of a serpent, and he may use this dreadful power. The abuse of greatness, or a great position, is when it separates human sympathy ("remorse") from power, is the next thought. And to speak the truth of Cæsar, Brutus admits, he has never known the time when Cæsar's emotions ("affections") overruled his reasoning power. Perhaps no finer tribute can be paid to a man's character or his mental balance than that he is not ruled by his emotions. This balance the historical Cæsar had markedly shown as early as when the punishment of the Catilinian conspirators was being discussed—and few had understood. But, Brutus goes on, it has often been proved that ambition just beginning to grow finds lowliness the first rung of a ladder. The climber first turns his face toward this ladder to ascend; but, once he has reached the top, he turns his back upon the steps by which he has mounted and looks to the clouds, scorning the humble rounds by which he reached his elevation. Cæsar may do this, he reflects, and so it must be prevented. Brutus, then, is willing that Cæsar should be killed, not for anything he has done but for what he might do. And, the speaker continues, since the accusation ("quarrel") can find no pretext ("bear no colour") in Cæsar's present character, it may be thought of, or fashioned, in this way: that his present position of power, if increased, might lead him to such and such extremes. And, therefore, it is best to think of him as a serpent's egg which, when hatched, will, like its kind, grow dangerous. It is best, then, to kill him in the shell. MacCallum, commenting on this speech, says, "Surely this argument is invented to support a foregone conclusion . . . 'Fashion it thus' betrays his resolve to make out a case." Then this writer asks, "Does the future contingency justify the infliction of death?" Granville Barker finds these the "thoughts of a solitary mind, unused to interplay with its fellows." And does not the solitary mind in its infrequent contacts often take on the color of other minds, and do we not seem to find here an echo of things Cassius may have said? The echo, to be sure, has taken on a poetic quality that Cassius could not give to it. In connection with this thought of the solitary mind, it should be noted that Shakespeare's time gave much attention to the effects of the secluded life because of the example of the religious mystics who abounded in the sixteenth century. Shakespeare was keenly interested in both the contemplative life and the active life, and gives us many comparative studies of the idealist and the practical man.

Brutus, then, we find, has been won over to the conspiracy—a conspiracy to assassinate a man who "besides being clothed with the sanctions of the law as the highest representative of the state, has been his personal friend and benefactor; all this, too, not on any ground of fact but on an assumed probability that the crown will prove a sacrament of evil, and transform him into quite another man. A strange piece of casuistry, indeed; but nowise unsuited to the spirit of the man who was to commit the gravest of crimes, purely from misplaced virtue. . . . Being such a man, of course he could only do what he did under some sort of delusion. . . . His great fault, then, lies in supposing it to be his duty to be meddling with things he does not understand." [2] Two things he failed to understand were: (1) that Rome needed a strong hand; and (2) that power in the hands of Julius Cæsar did not and could not mean tyranny.

If we could have tarried a few moments in Brutus' study after Lucius had lighted the taper, we should have discovered, on examining the labels, a copy of Plato's *Republic*. In this favorite "book" Brutus had found a thorough discussion of various forms of government. He had studied the learned discussion of tyranny and the tyrant. He had found such lines as these: "At first in the early days of his power, he is full of smiles, and he salutes everyone whom he meets, . . . making promises in public and also in private, liberating debtors, and distributing land to the people and his followers and wanting to be so kind and good to everyone! But when he has disposed of his foreign enemies by conquest and treaty and there is nothing to fear from them, then he is always stirring up some war or other, in order that the people may require a leader." Perhaps we do not won-

[2] Hudson.

der that poor Brutus was at sea—so mentally tossed about by Plato and Cassius! Theoretically he hated tyranny more than anyone in Rome. He was an easy prey for the person, or persons, who hated a man they wanted to think was a tyrant. And Brutus loved Rome. Above all Brutus loved Rome. His love for Rome and his regard for her future had come to resemble a spiritual ideal.

Lucius re-enters and, after announcing that the taper is burning in the study, he tells his master that, while searching about the window for a flint, he had found a sealed paper. Lucius is sure the paper was not there when he went to bed—and we know that Cinna has carried out Cassius' instructions. Brutus takes the letter and tells Lucius to get to bed again as it is not yet day. Then he thinks of the date and asks the boy if to-morrow is not the Ides, or fifteenth, of March. Lucius does not know, and Brutus sends him to look at the calendar—the calendar Julius Cæsar had given to the world. Lucius goes out and Brutus turns to the letter, saying that the "exhalations" whizzing in the air give enough light for reading. "Exhalations" usually meant meteors in Shakespeare's time. If it were not for the word "whizzing" one would prefer to accept the definition "short bursts" and refer it to flashes of lightning. The word "whizzing" applies to meteors more satisfactorily than to lightning. However, as the *New Clarendon* edition notes, "The words serve to remind the audience that the scene is supposed to be at night, although it is being acted by daylight!" Brutus opens the letter and reads, by an intermittent light, Cassius' anonymous charge that he is asleep, which is followed by the admonition to awake and see himself, to speak, to strike, to redress. This, as we know, is a repetition of what Cassius has said to him and should give him a clue to the identity of the writer. Brutus pauses to say that such "instigations" have often been dropped where he has taken them up. From the beginning he has recognized that he is being worked upon. Shall Rome, he reads on, piecing it out as the light permits, shall Rome stand under one man's awe? What! Rome?, he exclaims, Rome in danger! His pride in his forebears awakens and he speaks of his ancestor who drove Tarquin from the streets of Rome when he was called king. Speak, strike, redress, he reads. Each of these words, it will be noticed, makes up a foot of the meter, giving a strong emphasis. Brutus wonders that he is entreated to speak and strike, but gives a solemn promise to Rome, warming up with an eloquent, "O Rome". If the redress shall follow this speaking and striking, then Rome will receive everything she has asked for ("thy full petition") from the hand of Brutus! So, as MacCallum points out, he takes these unsigned instigations for the voice of Rome, when they are the fabrications of a single schemer. This author continues, "He would not be Brutus if he suspected or shirked the summons. . . . This platonic theorist can easily be hoodwinked by the practical politician. So Brutus, who is so at home in his study with his books, who is so exemplary in all his private relations of friend, master, and husband, predestined, one would say, for the serene labors of philosophic thought and the gracious offices of domestic affection, sweeps from his quiet anchorage to face the storms of political strife, which such as he are not born to master, but which they think they cannot avoid."

Lucius returns with the information that fourteen days of March have passed. A knocking at the outer gate is heard and Brutus sends Lucius to answer. This knocking has not been commented upon as is the knocking at the south entry of Inverness Castle, but it is almost as effective in that we sense that some evil thing is about to enter. The ancient world had a strong belief that evil is abroad at night, and Shakespeare uses the thought frequently. (The shadowy forms of the conspirators in the storm have been like the personifications of evil things.) G. Wilson Knight [3] compares the speech that follows with Macbeth's soliloquy which begins, "These supernatural solicitings" (I, III, 130) and says, "The state of evil endured by Macbeth is less powerfully, but similarly, experienced by Brutus. Its signs are loneliness, a sense of unreality, a sickly vision of nightmare forms. It contemplates murder and anarchy to symbolize outwardly its own inner anarchy." Brutus now speaks of this inner anarchy as he waits for Lucius to answer the knocking at the gate. He begins by saying that he

[3] In *The Wheel of Fire.*

has not slept since Cassius began to incite him against Cæsar. Then he reflects that between the execution of a dreadful thing and its first conception all the intervening time is like a wild vision ("phantasma") or a hideous dream. The spirit that controls a man's destiny ("genius") and his own emotions ("mortal instruments") are in council, or debate, and a man's condition is similar to that of a little kingdom which is undergoing an insurrection. The above reading of the word "genius" is the one accepted by most critics. However, "genius" in the Roman religion was "the indwelling spirit of a man which gave him the power of generation. . . . This notion grew somewhat wider and the *genius* came to denote all the full powers of developed manhood. . . . The corresponding spirit in woman was known as 'Juno'. . . . The word in classical usage had apparently nothing approaching the usual modern English sense of the word: exalted intellectual power in a person." [4] Some critics interpret "genius" as mind and "mortal instruments" as physical powers, thus using the modern meaning of "genius."

Going back to Brutus' thought about insurrections, it should be noted that, in his *Plato,* Brutus had read, "Let me ask you not to forget the parallel of the individual and the state," and, "He will look at the city which is within him and take heed that no disorder occur in it." How literally Brutus has applied his philosophy! Before leaving this section of the scene

[4] *Oxford Companion to Classical Literature.*

it may be well to recall that, while Brutus accepted the letters as representing the voice of Rome, he had already made up his mind before reading them, and it was largely on Cassius' insistence that the decision was made. This tells a great deal about Brutus' confidence in Cassius and, less directly, suggests quite strongly an evidence of Cassius' former honor and trustworthiness.

Lucius returns with the information that the master's brother is at the door. (Cassius was married to Brutus' sister.) Brutus asks if Cassius is alone and is told that more are with him, men with their hats (or hoods, as they would be in Rome) pulled down about their ears and with half their faces buried in their cloaks. Lucius is unable to recognize any of them by any distinguishing mark or feature of countenance ("favor"). Brutus tells him to admit the group, recognizing them as the faction. He then soliloquizes as follows, speaking to personified Conspiracy: Art thou ashamed, Conspiracy, he asks, to show thy dangerous brow at night when evils are free to roam about? O, then, when daylight comes, where wilt thou find a cavern dark enough to hide thy monstrous face? Seek no such hiding-place, Conspiracy, but conceal thy facial expression with smiles and affability. For if thou dost walk about ("path") wearing thy natural monstrous expression, not even the darkest cavern in hell (Erebus) is dim enough to hide thee from detection and frustration. Is it not evident here that, in spite of all his efforts to reconcile himself to the thought of the conspiracy, once he meets the actual deception and the covertness of it, he is shocked so that he shrinks instinctively from the hideousness of the plan? Brutus has been working the thing out as a problem, a theory, and has not anticipated the trickery and the lurking, stealthy secrecy involved, concealment from which his innate nobility recoils.

Six conspirators enter. (History tells us there were sixty in the plot.) Cassius speaks, with a courteous apology for intruding on Brutus' rest, greets him with a good-morning and hopes they are not disturbing him. Brutus replies that he has been up for an hour and has been awake all night. He then asks if the men who have accompanied Cassius are known to him, and Cassius answers that he knows all of them, adding that there is no man of them who does not honor Brutus. Every one of the men, he continues further, wishes that Brutus had the high opinion of himself that every noble Roman holds of him. Here we find another echo of things the speaker has said before. Cassius begins presenting his companions, announcing Trebonius first. Trebonius had been with Cæsar in Gaul, a trusted officer, and one wonders at his presence here among the conspirators. Froude tells us that Trebonius "had misconducted himself in Spain and was smarting under the recollection of his own failure." Brutus welcomes Trebonius, and Cassius next presents Decius Brutus. The other three, Casca, Cinna, and Metellus Cimber, are presented

in a group and all are made welcome. Brutus asks
what cares are preventing their sleep, but Cassius,
without making answer, draws him aside and they
converse in whispers. The others discuss the coming
of day and try to locate the place where the sun will
rise. Decius points out the direction he thinks is east
but Casca disagrees. Cinna begs his pardon and
agrees with Decius. He finds confirmation of his
opinion in the gray streaks that make bars, or fret-
work, across the sky. These lines are harbingers of
day, he says, but Casca informs them that they are
both wrong. Here, where he points his sword, the
sun rises. The sun is still toward ("growing on") the
south, allowing for ("weighing") the youthful sea-
son of the year, but in two months more (May) he
will rise, or present his fire, farther north. The high
east stands in the direction of the Capitol, where the
speaker now points. This conversation may seem
trivial, and is trivial, intended to be so by Shakespeare
to serve as a suggestion of their uneasiness.

Cassius has clinched his argument, played his last
card and, perhaps, outlined the general plans for the
assassination of Julius Cæsar on the morrow. Brutus
turns to the other conspirators with the earnest request that they give him their hands again. Cassius
injects the suggestion that they swear their resolution,
but Brutus says, No, not an oath, and continues, If
the "face" of men, with all that our souls have endured, and the abuses of the times are not strong
enough motives to bind us together—the sentence is

broken off at the word "abuse" and the speaker re-casts it. If, he goes on, these things which he has named are weak motives, then they should break off their conference early ("betimes") and go to their unoccupied beds. The word "face" at the beginning of the speech has been challenged and given several interpretations. The words "fate" and "faith" have been substituted. Those who accept "face" (which appears in the *First Folio*) interpret it, at Johnson's suggestion, as meaning "the countenance, the regard, the esteem of the public; in other terms, honour and reputation; or the 'face of men' may mean the dejected look of the people." Mason, rejecting Dr. Johnson's reading of the line, finds the word "faith" supported by the following passages of the speech, and adds "Brutus considered the faith of men as their firmest security in each other." [5] If these motives are too weak, Brutus continues, and they do go back to their beds, it will be to let high aspiring, or arrogant, tyranny range on until one by one the Romans are killed by proscription. But if his enumerated reasons bear fire enough, or inspiration enough (as he him-self is confident they do) to kindle cowards and to stiffen the weak spirits of women with valor, then what do they, who are most interested, need besides their own cause to spur them to redress their injuries? What other bond do they need, he asks, than that they are Romans who have given their word in a

[5] See, also, *Furness Variorum* for further discussion and other view-points.

secret conference and will not resort to trickery ("pal-
ter") ? And what other oath do they need but the
word of one honorable man to another ("honesty to
honesty") pledged ("engaged") to see the thing
through or fall for their cause? The speaker becomes
even more earnest as he urges that they may swear
priests and cowards, and crafty, deceitful ("caute-
lous") men, or men so old that they have become
more like corpses than human beings, and those poor
souls that are so inured to suffering that they mor-
bidly welcome more wrong. It may be proper to
swear all such untrustworthy people to their bad
causes, he grants, but they should not, he warns, stain
the flawless ("even") virtue of their present enterprise nor the unconquerable mettle of their spirits
by thinking that their cause, or their performance of
the deed, needs an oath, when every drop of blood a
noble Roman has in his body becomes guilty of a separate bastardy if he breaks the smallest particle of any
promise he has made. MacCallum finds this a "magnificent speech that breathes the true spirit of virtue
and conviction". He notes how Brutus has advanced
by leaps and bounds. Continuing, he says, "A few
minutes ago there was no complaint against Cæsar
as he was or had been, but it could be alleged that
he might change; now his tyranny, lighting by caprice on men, is announced as a positive fact of the
future, or even of the present. But by this time Brutus
is assured that the plot is just and that the confederates are the pick of men, both plot and confederates

so noble that for them the ordinary pledge would be an insult."

Brutus has won his argument and they abandon the oath. As Edward Dowden puts it, he has carried his point "by mere force of moral authority." One might add that the oratory is persuasive, too. Cassius now asks if they shall sound Cicero, and is of the opinion that he will stand strongly on their side. Casca adds eagerly that Cicero should not be left out and Cinna adds a decided, or perhaps echoing, "By no means." Metellus speaks at greater length and urges the inclusion of Cicero, arguing that this older man's silver hairs will gain the favor of the people and win their verbal approval.[6] It shall be said, the speaker adds, that Cicero's more mature judgment ruled their actions so that their younger impulsiveness shall not appear, but will be hidden by the elder man's gravity. Brutus is very definite in his opposition to such a plan, giving as his reason that Cicero will never follow anything that other men have begun, and asking that they do not impart anything to ("break with") him. Behind this brief sentence Gervinus finds an interesting revelation of Brutus' character. Brutus, he reminds us, possessed, like Hamlet, a cultivated mind and he "could not endure the Ciceros (Tullus and his brother), men whose cultivation advantaged nothing, whose finest principles were never living ones." This author comments fur-

[6] The *Arden* editors call attention to the play upon the words "silver" and "purchase".

ther, "Cæsar must fall as a sacrifice to his country, its weal and its freedom; necessity not hatred, justice not personal feeling, arm those hands against him. . . . No impure motive, such as Cicero's ambition, is to be permitted." Cassius agrees very readily to the exclusion of Cicero, although he had been the first to raise the question. Quiller-Couch tells us [7] that Cassius mistrusted Cicero on other grounds. He then adds, " 'No, indeed, he won't do,' chimed in Casca, ready as usual to contradict himself and echo the last speaker." Decius asks if no one else is to be assassinated with Cæsar and Cassius finds the question "well urged."

He expresses the opinion that Mark Antony, whom Cæsar loves, should not be permitted to outlive Cæsar. Antony, he adds, will be found to be a shrewd schemer and a cunning plotter and if he makes use of his position with the means at his disposal, he may become an annoyance or an inconvenience, perhaps a harmful one, to them. In order to prevent this Cassius thinks Antony should fall with Cæsar.

Brutus interposes with the objection that the course they are taking will then seem too bloody. They would be cutting the head off and then hacking the limbs, for Antony is but a limb of Cæsar. It would be like killing in anger and showing vindictiveness after. Then, addressing Cassius and calling him by his given name, he urges that they be sacrificers and not butchers. It must be remembered that this was a time

[7] In *Historical Tales from Shakespeare.*

when religious sacrifices were made. Brutus sees Cæsar as an offering and the assassination as a ritualistic act. Often in those days men sacrificed their dearest possession for a religious ideal. We are all opposed to the spirit of Cæsar, the idealist goes on, and there is no blood in the spirit of men. He expresses the wish that they might get at the spirit of Cæsar without dismembering the body. (Later we shall find him discovering that the death of the body did not kill the spirit.) But, alas, Cæsar must bleed, Brutus grants with deep regret. He addresses himself to the group of "gentle friends" with the suggestion that they kill Cæsar boldly but not wrathfully, that they carve him as a dish fit for the gods and not cut him up as a carcass fit for hounds. Let our hearts urge our hands to do this deed and then chide them for it afterwards, as subtle masters do with their children, is his next suggestion. Does this not reveal a mind unacquainted with subtlety, a mind almost childish in its simplicity? All this will make their plan necessary and not spiteful, Brutus continues; and, when it so appears to the eyes of the common man, the conspirators will be called purgers and not murderers. G. Wilson Knight tells us [8] that to Brutus "Cæsar's death is demanded not by man's envy and greed, but a divine necessity". As to Mark Antony, Brutus enjoins the others, think no further of him, for he can do no more than Cæsar's arm when Cæsar's head is off.

The practical, shrewd Cassius admits that he is

[8] In *Principles of Shakespearean Production.*

afraid of Antony because of the deep-rooted love he bears to Cæsar. How absolutely right he is will appear later. But Brutus interrupts before Cassius can finish, begging Cassius not to think of Antony. If he loves Cæsar all he can do is what he may do to himself—commit suicide through his regret at Cæsar's death. And that would be too much to expect of him because he is so fond of living—of sports, wildness and much company. Trebonius speaks for the first time with the opinion that there is no need to fear Antony, that he will live and laugh over the event in future instead of committing suicide. Trebonius and Antony were together in Gaul. It will be evident, as the play unfolds, that Cæsar had discovered Antony's nobler side, while Trebonius, as we learn here, had found only his lighter side—which tells a great deal about Trebonius.

A clock "strikes" three in the Elizabethan theatre, but there were no striking clocks in Rome, where water-clocks were used. It is Brutus who calls attention to the passing of time, and his word "Peace" might suggest that Trebonius' speech had jarred on him. Cassius knows the exact time. Trebonius, feeling no particular responsibility for the completion of the plans, says it is time to part, but Cassius, unwilling to leave anything in doubt, tells them it is uncertain whether Cæsar plans to come to the Senate. Casca knows that Cæsar has sent word to Cicero of his intention to attend and he might have interrupted here, but the impetuous Cassius is going on, saying

that Cæsar has grown superstitious of late, quite contrary to the strong opinions or convictions he has held
heretofore, convictions that put no credence in fan-
tasy, dreams, and ceremonies. It may be, the speaker
observes, that these portents ("prodigies"), which
are apparent to all, and the stormy, terrifying night
together with the persuasion of auguries may keep
him from the Capitol to-day.

The subject of Cæsar's superstition "craves wary
walking" by the commentator, for the reason that
many editors and critics accept the word of Cassius
here, which history does not bear out. Why anyone
should believe, without careful questioning, a speaker
so evidently prejudiced is difficult to understand, but
the fact remains that they do. Brutus is not the only
one Cassius convinced! Cassius, as we know, has
dwelt on the evidences of Cæsar's waning physical
strength with unsympathetic exaggeration, omitting
to mention Cæsar's earlier record as expert swimmer
and rider. There has been no mention of such incidents as the one when Cæsar ate rancid oil on his
salad without a wry face out of consideration for his
hostess. Now Cassius accuses him of being superstitious. The Epicureans stressed the elimination of
superstition and all belief in supernatural intervention. Cassius has become fanatical on the subject, as
we observed in his conduct during the storm. Cæsar
knew this, as evidenced in his aside to Antony in
Act I. It would be the nastiest thing Cassius could
say about Cæsar, according to his tenets, to accuse

him of superstition, and he cleverly connects it with the present problem and uses it as a trump card, a final belittling of Cæsar in the mind of Brutus. He makes the superstition a recent falling off and one wonders whether in doing this he is not afraid his statement will be challenged because of Cæsar's well-known freedom from superstition. Perhaps, too, he is giving himself credit for observing something the others have not seen. However [and this "however" might modify much of what has been said on Cassius' introduction of Cæsar's supersition], Cassius may be referring to a recent action of Cæsar's which was interpreted by the many as superstition. Baring-Gould throws this light on the subject which offers sufficient explanation of the incident: "A sneer has been cast at him (Cæsar) for ascending the steps of the temple of Jupiter on the Capitol at his triumph upon his knees, as a piece of grovelling superstition; but of superstition there was no trace in Cæsar's mind. It is far more probable that in the day of his highest glory he felt that all he had and all he had done were due to the protection of the All-Father, that mysterious, undefined, unrevealed, yet acknowledged Providence which a man of his genius and earnestness of mind could hardly fail to believe in, and that he desired to testify this by this outward act." Shakespeare's own testimony on the subject is found in Cæsar's rejection of the Soothsayer and his warning. Things that mean superstition to us, such as the runners touching women at the Lupercal games and the consulting of augurers, were accepted by all Romans and were questioned by no one, except possibly Cæsar, himself. Moulton finds an explanation for Cæsar's apparent superstition in the changed conditions he found in Rome on his return. "Politics", this author says, "had passed from science to gambling. . . . To come back to a world of which you have mastered the machinery and to find that it is no longer governed by machinery at all, that causes no longer produce effects,—this, if anything, might well drive a strong intellect to superstition." [9]

Decius speaks and tells Cassius not to fear; then he brags that, even if Cæsar had so resolved, he can persuade him to come. This is a blatant boast that he is willing to take advantage of Cæsar's confidence in him. Cæsar, he goes on, loves to hear tales about deceptions that are practiced on unsuspecting animals, when the tales are paralleled by stories of men who are deceived by flatterers. The betrayal of the animals mentioned is as follows: The unicorn was supposed to be captured by a huntsman who stood against a tree and stepped aside as the animal charged so that it drove its horn into the tree. Several explanations are given of "bears with glasses," all of which have to do with distracting the bear's attention with mirrors and affording his pursuers a surer aim. Elephants were trapped into pits lightly

[9] *Shakespeare as a Dramatic Artist.*

covered over with brush on which proper bait had been placed. Now, Decius boasts, he is going to trap Cæsar, as one lures an animal, by telling him he hates flatterers, when in truth he only says he does and is most flattered by being thought immune to flattery. "Let me work", the speaker goes on confidently, adding that he can give Cæsar's mood the right direction and will bring him to the Capitol. Moulton [10] finds this speech—and not the assassination of Cæsar—the "deepest tragedy of the play." Brutus must have been "noble" indeed not to see through Decius. Cassius seems exceptionally honest by comparison with Decius.

Cassius, as if unwilling to leave too much of the glory or the responsibility to Decius, declares that they will all be there to accompany Cæsar. Brutus asks if the eighth hour is the latest time for the assembly and Cinna suggests that they make that the limit and warns them not to fail the hour. Metellus Cimber speaks for the first time and suggests that they include Caius Ligarius in their group. He wonders that none of the others has thought of him when they know Cæsar dislikes him and alienated him by scolding ("rated") him for speaking well of Pompey. Brutus begs Metellus to go past the house of Ligarius and send Ligarius to him. He loves me well, the speaker says, and I have given him good reason for loving me. Brutus ends the speech by saying he will mould Ligarius to their purpose ("fashion him").

[10] In *Shakespeare as a Dramatic Artist.*

Cassius reminds them that the morning is coming upon them, and cautions them all to remember what they have said, or promised, and to show themselves true Romans. Brutus adds that they must all look fresh and merry and not let their facial expression, or looks, wear openly, or reveal, their designs. They must conduct themselves, or bear their part, as their Roman actors do, with untired spirits and dignified firmness of appearance ("formal constancy").[11] Again we turn to the historian where we find this comment: "No stronger evidence is needed of the demoralization of the Roman Senate than the completeness with which they were able to disguise from themselves the baseness of their treachery." [12]

The conspirators go out, and Brutus calls to Lucius. There is no response and Brutus says, It is no matter. He speaks to the boy, telling him to enjoy the sweet, honey-heavy, refreshing dew-like slumber since he has none of the visions or hallucinations which busy Care pictures in the minds of men. The part of Lucius is often played by a woman and most of us can readily agree with Granville Barker that "this is an abomination."

Portia enters. "Her appearance is admirably contrived. The conspirators are gone, Brutus is alone again, and the night's deep stillness is recalled. . . . But so softly she comes that for all the stillness he is

[11] *The New Clarendon Shakespeare* notes that "This is one of the rare favorable references to acting in Shakespeare. Most of his references to actors of his own time are unfavorable."
[12] Froude.

unaware of her until her soft voice barely breaking it says,

Brutus, my lord!" [13]

Brutus turns with surprise and a kindly rebuke for her early rising and exposing her delicate health to the raw, cold morning. Portia reminds him that he, too, is risking exposure, then she goes straight to the question in her mind. He has ungently stolen from her bed—"ungently," not taking care about disturbing her—and last night at supper he suddenly arose and walked about with his arms folded, pondering over something and sighing. And when she asked him to explain he had stared at her with ungentle looks. When she urged him further he had scratched his head and stamped impatiently with his foot. Still she insisted but he refused to answer and waved her out of his presence. She had left the room, fearing to increase his impatience that was already highly kindled, and hoping it was but the effect of "humour" which at some time has its hour with every man. "Humour" in Shakespeare's time referred to what were supposed to be the four chief fluids of the body (blood, phlegm, cheer, melancholy), the changing proportions of which affected a person's physical and mental life. This "humour" or unbalanced condition, Portia continues, will not let him eat or talk or sleep. If it could accomplish as great a change in his physical appearance as it has in his mental condition, she

[13] Granville Barker.

would not recognize him. However, some modern editors interpret "humours" more simply as merely "mood" or "caprice". Portia then begs her husband to make her acquainted with his grief. Brutus replies briefly that he is not well and that is all, but his wife meets the statement with the persuasive argument that he is wise and, if he were not well, he would embrace the means that would restore him to health. Brutus declares that he has done so and begs her to go back to bed. But Portia will not be put off. If he is ill, she insists, is it healthful ("physical") to walk unbuttoned and inhale the moisture ("humours") of the damp morning? If Brutus is sick, she asks, why does he steal out of his wholesome bed and risk the vile contagions of the night air [14] and defy the dampness that causes rheumatism? No, she concludes, her Brutus has some hurt ("sick offence") in his mind which by right and virtue of her place she should know of. She kneels and entreats ("charms") him by her own once-commended beauty, by all the vows of love, particularly their marriage vows, that he unfold to her, his other self, why he is so heavily burdened or oppressed, and what men have been received by him. She then admits frankly that she has been watching and has seen six or seven men enter in the darkness, hiding their faces. Brutus begs her not to kneel, addressing her as "gentle Portia," perhaps feeling unworthy of her devotion, and she tells

[14] It was commonly supposed in Shakespeare's time that night air was unwholesome.

him she would not need to kneel if he, too, were gentle. Her feeling deepens as she begs to know of him whether it comes within the marriage bond that she should know none of the secrets that concern him. She asks if she is a part of him but only within limitations, to keep him company at his meals, comfort his bed and talk to him occasionally. She reconstructs her expression of the thought and asks if she dwells only in the suburbs of his good pleasure. *The New Temple Shakespeare* has this note on the word "suburbs": "The phrase begins, as it were, by meaning no more than its face value, i.e., 'in the outskirts of your affection'. But the suburbs were traditionally the haunts of prostitutes and this *double entendre* led up to and is certainly emphasized by line 287." If this is so, Portia continues, then she is only Brutus' mistress and not his wife.

Brutus is deeply moved and assures her solemnly and tenderly that she is his true and honorable wife, as dear to him as the "ruddy drops" that "visit" his sad heart. "Some have seen in these two lovely lines an anticipation of Harvey's discovery of the circulation of the blood made public shortly after Shakespeare's death." [15] Portia's "If this were true" does not necessarily mean that she doubts his word, but that she wishes to impress on him all that their love means to her. A love as dear as his life-blood, according to her viewpoint, would admit her to his confidence. She grants that she is only a woman, she con-

[15] *The New Clarendon Shakespeare.*

tends, still ("withal") she is the woman Lord Brutus took for his wife. She repeats her, "I grant I am a woman" and this time adds that she is a woman of good repute and the daughter of Cato. She knew her husband's high regard for Cato who was his uncle, his mother's half-brother. Brutus had grown up in the household of Cato. Professor Max Radin, in his life of Brutus, calls Cato the man who moulded Brutus. Cato was "a man of unbending character and absolute integrity, narrow, short-sighted, impervious to reason as to bribery." [16] Professor Radin tells us, "The solemn boy was thrilled to a passionate admiration by the figure of the unsmiling Stoic pouring his soul into statements of principles and into denunciation of those who wished to guide the state without principles." And the boy was influenced by Cato to partake in active political life for which he had no fitness. To continue with Radin, "An ideal was set before him by a stronger personality than his own, and this ideal became so fully the purpose of his life that he never questioned its superiority to the one that would have really gratified the longing of his heart." Cato had been on the side of the Senate in the wars between Cæsar and Pompey. After the death of Pompey and the loss of the cause, he took his own life—as we know his daughter will do before the end of the play. Portia is proud of the fortitude she has inherited from her father and now asks if she is not stronger than others of her sex, since she is so fath-

[16] *Oxford Companion to Classical Literature.*

ered and so husbanded. She knows her pleading has moved her husband now, and she asks again that he tell her his secrets, promising that she will not disclose them. She tells him of the proof to which she has put her resolution and endurance. She has given herself a voluntary wound in the thigh, and she points to the place.[17] She concludes by asking if she can bear such suffering with patience and secrecy and not keep her husband's secrets. Brutus is overcome and prays the gods to make him worthy of this noble wife. "Brutus, touched and amazed by his wife's heroism, took her in his arms and would have told her the whole story then and there but a knocking interrupted him, and with a hurried promise that she should know all he dismissed her into the house just as the boy admitted the last of the conspirators."[18] Brutus has promised that he will explain all his engagements to her and all the story that has been written upon his sad brow. Dowden finds that "No relation of man and woman in the plays of Shakespeare is altogether so noble as that of Portia and Brutus."[19]

Lucius enters, presenting "a sick man". Brutus recognizes Ligarius and asks Lucius to stand aside that he may reach him and grasp his hand. The question, "How?" probably expresses his surprise at finding Ligarius wearing a kerchief over his head

[17] Radin tells us there is no reason to doubt this famous story.

[18] Quiller-Couch—*Historical Tales from Shakespeare.*

[19] Shakespeare ignores the historical fact that both Brutus and Portia had been married before. Portia's first husband was Bibulus, who had served as consul with Julius Cæsar and been completely overshadowed by him.

which, in Shakespeare's time, was a sign of illness. Ligarius asks Brutus to receive ("vouchsafe") a "good morning" from a feeble tongue and Brutus exclaims at the unfortunate circumstance of Ligarius being ill at this time. But Ligarius declares that he is not sick if Brutus has in hand any exploit worthy of the name of honor. Brutus admits that he has some such enterprise on hand and would tell it if Ligarius were well enough to hear. Ligarius declares by all the gods the Romans worship that he will here discard his sickness. Then addressing Brutus as "the soul of Rome" and a brave son of Rome descended from honorable forebears, tells him that like a conjuror ("exorcist") [20] he has charmed into activity his (Ligarius') apathetic spirits. Now Brutus may even bid him run, and he will strive to do things that have seemed impossible of performance. Yea, he adds with enthusiasm, he will get the better of those insurmountable things. Eagerly he asks what there is to do. In Plutarch's story Brutus goes to Ligarius and Ligarius gets up from a sick-bed to join the conspirators. Shakespeare keeps most of Plutarch's phrasing, but builds up the character of Brutus by showing Ligarius more eager and making that eagerness dependent on his loyalty to Brutus. Brutus answers the question of Ligarius by saying there is a piece of work to do that will restore all sick men to health. Metellus may have given Ligarius a hint of the conspiracy when he

[20] Mason says, "Here and in all other places when the word occurs in Shakespeare, to *exorcise* means to raise spirits, not to lay them; and, I believe, he is singular in his acceptance of it."

stopped by with Brutus' message, for Ligarius now asks if there are not some men "whole", or well, who must be made sick. Brutus agrees that what Ligarius hints must be done, but adds that he will explain to whom it is to be done as they are on their way. Are we not relieved not to hear Brutus expound the conspiracy to Ligarius, or to anyone? Time has been condensed here. The interview of Portia and Brutus would not have filled the interval between the departure of the conspirators and the time for going to Cæsar's house before the meeting of the Senate. Ligarius boldly bids Brutus set his foot, or start immediately and he will follow with a heart newly enkindled. He does not know, he adds, what is to be done, but it is enough for him that Brutus leads him. Brutus asks him to follow and we may assume that, during the last part of the conversation, he has changed from his robe to his toga or rain cape.

Cæsar, too, will soon be on his way to the Senate. But can the conspirators do any greater injury to him than they have done to Brutus?

ACT II—SCENE II

On that stormy night that was to be the last of his life, while the conspirators were skulking about the streets of Rome, Julius Cæsar had dined with M. Æmilius Lipidus. After the meal, while the company conversed, Cæsar excused himself to look over some papers. Plans were already made for him to embark on the campaign into Parthia. The eighteenth was the date set and in three days he expected to be on his way. But there were still things to be done, including documents to be signed. The conversation about him turned to the subject of death and the speakers were discussing the question, What kind of death seems preferable? Cæsar, whose powers of attending to a number of things at one time were very marked, looked up from his papers and said, "A sudden one." A little later he went home, accompanied no doubt by Casca. Cæsar slept better than Brutus had done, but Calpurnia was nervous and restless. They arose at the usual time. Calpurnia dressed and went to look about the household, perhaps to the servants' quarters, where she found tales of the night's events. Cæsar threw on his night-robe, probably over his tunic, and went into the atrium, a room corresponding to the modern living room or drawing room.

As Cæsar enters, the storm is still raging and he

remarks that neither heaven nor earth has been at peace to-night. Even this brief line is significant in that it seems to suggest his love for peace. However, the critics do not stress this point, if they observe it. They seem to be divided as to whether it expresses his sympathy for Calpurnia or his own nervous apprehension. Cæsar goes on to say that three times Calpurnia had cried out in her sleep for help, exclaiming that Cæsar was being murdered. He goes to the door, calls a servant and tells him to go to the priests and bid them do immediate ("present") sacrifice and then bring him their opinion of success for the day's venture. This reading is borne out by Cæsar's reply on the return of the servant with the report of the augury. For this reason it seems better than the interpretation which sees him inquiring as to the outcome of his political plans. "The object of the Roman augury, and of divination in general, was not so much to ascertain the future as to secure that the favor of the gods was with them in the business at hand—to put it bluntly to get the luck on their side." [1] A few lines farther down we shall find Cæsar disregarding the augury.

Calpurnia has heard enough of the conversation as she enters to know that Cæsar contemplates attending the meeting. She exclaims in surprise, asking what he means, if he is thinking of walking forth in the storm. Then she declares that he shall not stir out of the house to-day. Cæsar announces his intention of going out, adding that the things that have

[1] *The Cambridge Ancient History.*

threatened him have been only the things that have tried to steal upon him from behind; when they have met him face to face they vanished. This, of course, is one of the speeches that some of the critics find boastful—a subject that will be discussed at the close of Act III when Shakespeare's presentation of Cæsar's character will be considered. Calpurnia replies, addressing him deferentially as "Cæsar" as a woman much younger than her husband might do, saying she never has insisted on the belief in ("stood on") superstitious observances ("ceremonies") but these supernatural happenings have frightened her. There is one "within", perhaps in the servants' quarters, who, besides the things they themselves have heard and seen, has told of most horrid sights seen by the night watchman. She repeats the story: A lioness gave birth to young in the streets; graves opened wide and gave up their dead; and fierce, fiery warriors were seen fighting on the clouds. These warriors were drawn up in military forms, in ranks and squadrons, and the blood from their battle drizzled down upon the Capitol; the noise of battle clashed ("hurtled") in the air; the neighing of horses was plainly heard; the groans of dying men reached the earth and ghosts went about the streets shrieking and squealing.[2] Calpurnia closes her speech by admitting again that she is afraid.

Some of the critics find the relationship between Cæsar and Calpurnia less affectionate (or "a shallow

[2] Homer believed that ghosts had thin, squeaking voices and compares them to the noise of bats disturbed in a cave.

relation"—Boas) than that between Brutus and Portia. Surely one would expect at first glance that Cæsar would reply to this speech with some words of comfort. But we must reflect that he doubtless has been reassuring her for some time, and that now the question on his mind is the meeting and his duty to attend. Any comparison between the two couples should take into consideration their respective ages. Brutus and Portia were near the same age. Cæsar is old enough to be Calpurnia's father. Do we not find in her attitude toward him a mixture of mother and daughter? Cæsar replies, asking what event can be avoided if it is purposed, or planned, by the mighty gods, and declaring again that he will go forth. These predictions, he adds, are to the world in general as well as to Cæsar. Calpurnia, we should note, has interpreted them as applying to Cæsar alone. Is not that exalting her husband above all men? She continues, arguing that when beggars die there is not even a shooting star seen (at least one would like to interpret the word "comet" so), but when a prince dies the very heavens blaze forth.

Cæsar speaks, and the student may be certain this speech has been much commented upon:

> *Cowards die many times before their deaths;*
> *The valiant never taste of death but once.*
> *Of all the wonders that I yet have heard*
> *It seems to me most strange that men should fear;*
> *Seeing that death, a necessary end,*
> *Will come when it will come.*

Plutarch says (with modernized spelling), "And when some of his friends did counsel him to have a regard for the safety of his person, and some did offer themselves to serve him, he would never consent to it, but said it was better to die once than always to be afraid of death." MacCallum says, on this speech, "His courage, of course, is beyond question; but is there not a hint of the theatrical in this overstrained amazement, and this statement that fear is the most unaccountable thing of all his experience?" Moulton says, almost as if in reply to the above comment, "But surely it must be possible for dramatic language to distinguish between the true and the assumed force; and equally surely there is a genuine ring in the speeches in which Cæsar's heroic spirit, shut from the natural sphere of action in which it has been so often proved, leaps restlessly at every opportunity into pregnant words. We may feel certain of his lofty physical courage." Then this writer quotes the lines of the speech above. To what extent Cæsar was a student of the philosophies we do not know. To be sure we have heard his opinion of Cassius and his tendency to read and think too much. However, Lucretius, an ardent believer in the Epicurean system of philosophy, had popularized those doctrines, laying greater stress than did his teacher on the folly of superstitious fear of the gods and the dread of death. His writings were so widely distributed and so much discussed that Cæsar scarcely could have avoided them. Unlike most Romans, however, he must have found an echo of his own thoughts in this philosophy that sought to dispel superstition and anxiety. The student should keep in mind that such matters as are found in this conversation were subject for daily discussion in Rome, when the early religions had lost their hold on the educated classes and general skepticism had been substituted. It was philosophy only that enabled men to meet their fate with fortitude, and we may rest assured that Julius Cæsar had gleaned the best from the teachings of the times, in addition to the personal philosophy he had worked out in the solitudes of Gaul and throughout his thoughtful lifetime.

The servant re-enters with the information that the auguries would not have Cæsar stir forth to-day. In plucking out the entrails of the offering they had found no heart in the beast. Cæsar says the gods do this to shame cowards. Then he declares that Cæsar himself would be a beast without a heart, or cowardly, if he should stay at home to-day merely out of fear. No, he says conclusively, he will not stay at home.[3] Cæsar speaks of Danger as a person and says that Danger knows full well that Cæsar is more dangerous than he. Cæsar and Danger are two lions littered in the same day, he continues, and Cæsar is the more terrible. He ends by repeating his determination to go forth. The historian [4] tells us that, "In

---

[3] Instead of finding Cæsar "urged by his anxiety to consult the oracles" as MacCallum has it, one is tempted to make the facetious remark that he may have attempted to get the oracles on his side against Calpurnia.

[4] Froude.

practice Cæsar treated the auguries with contempt. He carried his laws in open disregard of them. He fought his battles, careless whether the sacred chicken would eat or the calves' livers were the proper color." Granville Barker finds "operatic sonority" in this speech. Chambers says, "It is noteworthy in the play that the impression it yields of Cæsar's greatness is largely afforded by his own self-conscious utterances. . . . This self-laudation, which is not perhaps wholly inconsistent with the view of Decius Brutus that Cæsar is 'then most flattered' when he is told that he hates flatterers, serves in its turn Shakespeare's dramatic purpose. . . . And none the less it carries conviction, as an estimate, not merely of what Cæsar would be taken to be, but of what he is." G. Wilson Knight observes, after quoting the above lines about danger, "He is conscious of his own triumphant destiny. . . . The idea of Cæsar is ever far greater here than Cæsar the man. It is so to Cæsar himself. He has an almost superstitious respect for his own star and is afraid of acting unworthy of it, thus he persuades himself not to show fear, since he is greater than Danger itself." And Moulton,[5] after quoting the passage comments, "A man must have felt the thrill of courage in search of its food, danger, before his self-assertion finds language of this kind to express itself."

Calpurnia tells her husband that his wisdom is eaten up by self-confidence. She begs him again not to go forth to-day. He may call it her fear and not

[5] In *Shakespeare as a Dramatic Artist.*

his own that keeps him in the house, she offers, and they will send Mark Antony to the Senate House to say that Cæsar is not well to-day. She drops on her knees before him and entreats him to let her have her way. Cæsar is moved and gives in, accepting her suggestion that Mark Antony shall say he is not well. At this point Decius Brutus enters, debonair, confident. Cæsar concludes his speech by saying to Calpurnia that Decius Brutus shall tell the Senate of his decision. Decius greets Cæsar obsequiously, addressing him as "worthy Cæsar" and adding that he has come to accompany Cæsar to the Senate House. Cæsar replies that it is at an opportune moment to bear his greeting to the Senate and to tell them that he "will not" come to-day. "Cannot", he adds, would be false, and "dare not" falser. "I will not come to-day," he concludes, and asks Decius to tell them so. Calpurnia puts in a word and asks Decius to say her husband is sick. Cæsar turns to her, perhaps a little sternly, and asks if Cæsar shall send a lie. He elaborates, asking if after all his conquests that have stretched his power to such great lengths he should be afraid to tell the truth to a group of graybeards. He instructs Decius again to deliver the message that he "will not" come.

Decius' first approach to his problem of winning Cæsar it clever. He begs "mighty Cæsar" to give him some reason for the decision lest he, the bearer of the message, be laughed at. Cæsar affirms stoutly that the reason lies in his will. He will not come, and that is enough to satisfy the Senate. For Decius' private satisfaction, and because he loves Decius, he will let him know the underlying reason: Calpurnia, his wife, wishes to detain him at home because of a dream she had last night. He describes the dream. She saw his statue and from it there ran pure blood, as if it were a fountain with a hundred spouts. And many lusty Romans came smiling and bathed their hands in the blood. Calpurnia has interpreted the dream as a warning, or portent, of evils that are imminent. She has begged him on her knees to stay at home to-day. Decius is ready with his argument and says, lightly, that the dream has been interpreted amiss. It was, rather, a fair and fortunate dream. The statue spouting blood from many pipes in which so many Romans bathed signifies that great Rome shall suck reviving blood from Cæsar. Professor Kittredge finds the last part of the sentence "a good instance of dramatic irony". This editor continues, "for Decius' interpretation, though accepted by Cæsar, sounds ominous enough. His language, however, is figurative—and so Cæsar understands it: Great men shall be eager for a share in the fresh life-blood of prosperity which your rule will infuse into the veins of Rome; and they shall throng about you for that share as eagerly as devotees press forward to dip their handkerchiefs in the blood of a martyr." On the following lines this author continues, "*Tinctures* and *stains* are synonymous. *Relics* suggests the relics of saints preserved in churches. *Cognizance* indicates an heraldic badge, worn to show that one belongs to the household of some great noble. Here it sums up the nouns that precede: 'for tinctures, stains, relics in a word, for a sign that they are devoted to Cæsar as the restorer of Rome'." The editors of *New Temple Shakespeare* find some confusion of thought here because "of these four words *cognizance* has normally a heraldic significance; *stains* and *relics* seem to refer rather to the habit of securing mementos of martyrs; *tinctures* is normally heraldic, but might be merely an equivalent for *stains*. It looks as though there were some confusion of thought, since on Decius' favorable interpretation of the dream the heraldic significance is much more appropriate to the *living* Cæsar, dispensing distinctions to 'great men', whereas the martyr significance is much more appropriate to what actually occurred."

Cæsar trustingly gives Decius credit for interpreting the dream well. Decius accepts the praise and says that Cæsar will agree when he hears what he has to say. He would have Cæsar know that the Senate has concluded to give a crown to Cæsar to-day. If the speaker should tell them that Cæsar will not come they may change their minds. Besides, the mocking remark is likely to be made that they should break up the mutiny of the Senate until another time when Cæsar's wife shall have better dreams. Or, if Cæsar thus hides away, are they not likely to whisper that he is afraid? He begs Cæsar's pardon and assures him that it is his own dear, dear love for

Cæsar's conduct or way of life ("proceeding") that bids him tell him all this. He ends with the apparently humble statement that his reason is subordinated to his love, or, as *The New Clarendon Shakespeare* puts it, "I am going beyond the bounds of prudence in speaking so freely but it is at the dictates of love." Professor Kittredge finds that "The hypocrisy of this speech goes beyond anything that we can pardon even in the most patriotic conspirator." And, this writer adds, "Shakespeare intends to make Decius hateful to us, and at the same time to show how blinded Cæsar is by self-confidence." Still, to Cæsar they are the words of a friend, a friend telling him that mocking remarks may be made about the influence of his wife's dreams on his official actions, telling him that the greybeards may think he is hiding away, afraid—Cæsar who should never be mocked, because of his integrity, Cæsar who has never been afraid. He turns to Calpurnia and admits that her fears seem foolish now and says he is ashamed that he yielded to them. In considering Cæsar's changing his decision, it should be kept in mind that a crown offered by the Senate had a far greater significance than a crown offered by a consul, no matter what group he might represent outside the Senate. Cæsar asks a servant, or perhaps his wife, to bring his robe or toga. The toga that is brought him is probably not the white one in which he usually presided over the Senate. Neither was it the heavy rain coat or cape that was used for inclement weather, but probably a toga of dark color and medium weight material—one that had seen service in his military campaigns. We shall learn more of this toga later.

The critics find inconsistency and vacillation in Cæsar's deciding to go to the Senate after his promise to his wife not to go. Some of their comments are very convincing. On the other side, however, the question may be asked, Does not the urgency of the business of presenting the crown seem sufficient reason for any conscientious man to change his mind? We need not accept the theory that Cæsar wanted the crown. He wanted to be present when the Senate chose to make the presentation. We do not know whether Cæsar wanted the crown. We do know that he recognized his obligation to the Senate.

Before leaving this part of the scene notice should be taken of Cæsar's frequent reference to himself in the third person, the using of his name in place of the first personal pronoun. Some critics find this manner of speech another evidence of Cæsar's "egotism" —Shakespeare's Cæsar is meant. Cæsar had used this form in his *Commentaries,* which Buchan describes (and others agree) as "the most unegotistic book ever written." "Egotism" is a word loosely used, a word that can easily be confused with self-confidence, the kind of self-confidence that has come out of a realization of certain accomplishments attained. But for a clear understanding of the meaning of the word "egotist" and the distinction between that word and "egoist" one must turn to the phychologist. William McDougall tells us: [6] "Egoism is inward; egotism lies in outward expression. The egoist is essentially selfish; he acts benevolently only in so far as, by so acting, he promotes his own interests; he is kind only to be comfortable. The egotist may be truly kind, and is more often amiable than hateful. Egoism is a deeply rooted moral defect; egotism is an offence against good taste."

A group of conspirators enters. Does Publius belong to the "faction"? Publius has entered first and Cæsar welcomes him as his escort; then he sees the others, and comments on Brutus being up so early, perhaps a reference to Brutus' habit of burning the midnight oil in his study. He says good morning to Casca and, noticing the effect of Ligarius' illness, tells him, with a kindly smile, that Cæsar was never so much his enemy [7] as the ague that has made him lean. Then he asks the time and Brutus gives the hour as eight o'clock. Cæsar thanks them cordially for the pains they are taking to escort him and for the courtesy they pay him. Antony enters and Cæsar remarks, perhaps jovially, that even the night-reveller is up early. His greeting to Antony is returned with a courteous reply to "most noble Cæsar." Cæsar goes to the door of the triclinium, or dining-room, and tells servants within to prepare refreshments. These would probably consist of bread and wine with olives,

---

[6] In *Character and the Conduct of Life.*
[7] Ligarius fought on the side of Pompey in the wars.

raisins, and cheese, which would very likely constitute Cæsar's breakfast.[8] The host apologizes for not
having been ready and assumes the blame for the
delay. Cinna, Metellus, and Trebonius arrive and
are greeted. Cæsar expresses surprise at seeing Trebonius, but goes on to tell him that he wishes to have
a talk of an hour's duration with him, and Trebonius
is to remind him of it and be near him so that he will
remember. One may wonder if this contemplated
interview had as its object a better understanding
with Trebonius over the affair in Spain, or whether
Cæsar intended to speak to him about the future
consulship that had been promised, and that Trebonius considered too distant a reward for his services. Trebonuis agrees aloud that he will remain
near Cæsar at his request, but aside he adds that he
will be so near that Cæsar's best friends will wish he
had been farther away. The servants have signified
their readiness and the gracious host bids his friends
go into the triclinium and taste some wine with him,
adding that then they all "like friends" will go to the
Senate together.

Brutus speaks aside, reflecting that his own heart
grieves ("yearns") to think that every "like" is not
the same, or everyone's conception of the words "like
friends" is not the same. There is a beautiful tribute
to Cæsar here, for the meaning seems to be that
Cæsar's friendship is true and the others', including

[8] See *The Roman's World*—Moore.

his own, is untrue. Is not Brutus still "at war" with himself?

It should be noted that Cassius is not present. On this important point Mark Hunter says, "Cassius is, indeed, honourably distinguished from the others in one respect. He is at least an open enemy. He makes no pretence of love for his victim, but at once distrusts and is distrusted. It is significant that he separates himself from the final act of treachery to which even Brutus stoops, and is the only conspirator who does not present himself at Cæsar's house on the morning of the Ides to partake of his hospitality, 'like a friend,' and then lead him forth to slaughter."

Thomas Davies comments as follows on Shakespeare's presentation of Cæsar in this scene: "There is scarcely any part of Cæsar's character so well understood and so happily expressed by Shakespeare as the great urbanity of his manners, and the ease and affability of his conversation. If Cæsar was the greatest soldier, he seems likewise to have been the best bred man of all antiquity. In this short scene his address varies with the character of the person to whom he speaks. The compliment he pays to Caius Ligarius is a happy mixture of politeness and humanity."

ACT II—SCENE III

ARTEMIDORUS, a Greek teacher of rhetoric, is shown on a street near the Capitol reading a letter that he has written to Cæsar. He announces his intention of standing where Cæsar will pass, when he will give him the letter. The letter warns Cæsar against the conspirators and admonishes that carelessness, or freedom from anxiety, opens the way for conspiracy. Continuing to speak, the Greek says his heart laments that virtue cannot live in the presence of envious rivalry ("emulation"). If Cæsar will read this letter he may live; if not, it must be that the Fates are conspiring with the traitors for his downfall.

"The scene serves to show that Cæsar had well-wishers, and to make the audience wonder whether the conspiracy may not be found out in time." [1]

[1] *New Clarendon*—Notes.

ACT II—SCENE IV

PORTIA is shown with Lucius before the house of Brutus. She is excitedly giving him instructions to go to the Senate House, with no mention of what is to be accomplished there. Lucius reminds her that he must know the object of his errand, but instead of enlightening him she says, nervously, that she wishes he could go and return in less time that it would take to tell him of the errand. Then she breaks out in an aside not intended for Lucius, begging that Firmness or Self-possession ("Constancy") may be strongly on her side; that Firmness may place a huge barrier between her heart and her tongue so that she will not reveal all that is now moving her. She has a man's mind, she reflects, but only a woman's physical strength. She exclaims on the difficulty a woman has in keeping a secret, then turns and, finding Lucius, is surprised that he is not gone. Lucius again reminds her that he has had no definite orders and asks if he is only to run to the Capitol and return. Portia pulls herself together enough to suggest that her anxiety is for her lord's health. Lucius is to go and notice if he looks well. Then her real anxiety comes out and she urges the boy to note what Cæsar is doing and what suitors, or petitioners, press about him. She thinks she hears a noise and with growing agitation

141

asks Lucius what it may be. The boy has heard nothing. Portia urges him to listen well, then describes the noise as being like the confused sounds ("bustling rumour") attending a fight or contention of some sort. Lucius again assures her that in truth ("sooth") he has heard no sound.

A Soothsayer enters and Portia accosts him, asking him to come nearer. She questions him as to where he has been (hoping he has come from the Capitol) and as to the time, then inquires if Cæsar has gone to the Capitol. The Soothsayer answers that he has come from his own house, that it is nine o'clock and that Cæsar has not gone to the Capitol. The speaker adds that he himself is going to find a place where he may see Cæsar pass. Portia asks if he has some petition for Cæsar, and the Soothsayer says he has an appeal for Cæsar if he will be good enough to hear. Then he adds the information that he is going to beseech Cæsar to befriend and protect himself. Portia asks the rather unguarded question whether the man knows any harm intended to Cæsar and is told that there is nothing the Soothsayer knows but much that he fears may happen. He bids the lady good-day, remarking that, since the street is narrow and there is such a throng following Cæsar, he must be going along or a feeble man like himself may be crushed almost to death; he will go and get himself a place where it is not so crowded so that he may speak to Cæsar as he comes along. The Soothsayer goes on his way and Portia, speaking aside that Lucius may not hear, exclaims on what a weak thing the heart of woman is. She speaks to her husband and prays that the heavens may speed him in his enterprise. "Murder is the enterprise, and Cato's daughter knows it. But he is her Brutus; so may the heavens speed him even in this." [1] Portia becomes conscious of Lucius' presence again and is certain he has heard. She starts to make an explanation to him, saying that her husband has a suit that Cæsar will not grant, but gives up and says, again aside, that she is growing faint. She returns to her first intention of learning through Lucius what has transpired and tells him to go and commend her to her lord. He is to say that she is merry and come back immediately with the answer. Lucius goes toward the Capitol and Portia turns indoors.

The door closes behind the wife of Brutus and she will be seen no more in the play. A few quotations from the commentators may be of assistance to the student in making his own estimate of the character.

"It is not Portia's fault that it [Brutus' communicating the secret to her] does not betray everything. When it comes to the point she can neither hold her tongue nor control herself. She betrays her anxiety and uneasiness to the boy Lucius, and herself exclaims,

'I have a man's mind but a woman's might.
How hard it is for women to keep counsel!'

[1] Granville Barker.

The reflection is obviously not Portia's but an utterance of Shakespeare's own philosophy of life, which he has not cared to keep to himself." [2]

"She overrated her woman's strength when she forced herself into the conspiracy, as he [Brutus] in his sphere overrated his powers when he placed himself at the head of the conspiracy." [3]

"Such a woman as Portia pays a terrible tax for her self-mastery. The chief payment of effusive tears and hysterical cries she cannot render as her tribute to the tyrannous powers. When tears escape her, each one is distilled with an intense agony. And because she yields less than others, she may snap more suddenly. 'It is the strongest hearts,' said Landon, 'that are soonest broken.' Had Portia been less her husband's equal, less absolutely one with him in his aims and endeavors, she might have lived. . . . Shakespeare, with fine judgment, has allowed us to see Portia seldom in the play; otherwise an interest alien from the one he intended might have grown predominant." [4]

"The delineation of Portia is completed in a few masterly strokes. Once seen, the portrait ever after lives an old and dear acquaintance of the reader's inner man. Like some women I have known, Portia has strength enough to do and suffer for others, but very little for herself. . . . She has a clear idea of the stoical calmness and fortitude which appear so noble and so graceful in her Brutus; it all lies faith-

[2] Brandes.   [3] Gervinus.   [4] Dowden.

fully reproduced in her mind; she knows well how to honour and admire it; yet she cannot work it into the texture of her character; she can talk it like a book, but she tries in vain to live it." [5]

"She has a great spirit, but it is lodged in a fragile and nervous frame. Does she make her words good? She gains her point, but her success is almost too much for her. She can endure pain but not suspense: like Brutus she is a martyr to her sense of what is right." This author adds that she is "not directly responsible" for the consequences of the deed but that they "none the less flow from the deed that she encouraged and approved." [6]

[5] Hudson.   [6] MacCallum.

ACT III—SCENE I

WE COME now to Shakespeare's presentation of "the most brutal and the most pathetic scene that profane history has to record." [1] The author just quoted continues, "It was, as Goethe has said, the 'most senseless deed that ever was done'. It was wholly useless, for it did not and could not save Rome from monarchy. It was cowardly and treacherous in all its details; and it was utterly wrong-headed, for it showed that the men who were guilty of it knew neither what liberty nor government meant."

As to the staging of the scene in the Elizabethan theatre, we find G. H. Cowling [2] telling us, "The scene opens in a street leading to the Capitol as Cassius' lines,

> 'What, urge you your petitions in the street?
> Come to the Capitol.'

clearly indicate. But a moment later the members of the procession are assembled inside the Capitol and Cæsar is asking,

> 'Are we all ready?'

. . . There is no break in the scene which would give an opportunity of carrying in the benches. The

[1] Fowler.
[2] In *Shakespeare and the Theatre* by members of the Shakespeare Association.

146

benches which converted the platform into the Senate House must have been on the stage in the interval between Acts II and III. I imagine them placed in two rows at right angles to the tiring-house within the posts supporting the heavens. But they were ignored until they were needed. The stage was a street as the procession advanced from one of the doors down the side of the platform, where the business of Artemidorus and the Soothsayer would take place; but it became the interior of the Senate House as soon as the procession had winded round the post into the center of the stage. . . . I need hardly say that there is no authority in the folios for the modern stage direction 'the Senate sitting above' and 'Cæsar goes up to the Senate House, the rest following', which seems to imply that the murder of Cæsar was effected in the balcony, an impossible situation. . . . The preliminaries in the street were acted on the outer stage, and then Cæsar and the conspirators passed up the stage, under the proscenium arch into the scene."

Cæsar recognizes the Soothsayer in the crowd and calls to him that the Ides of March are come, and the reply is quick and ominous—that the day is not gone. (This incident is historical.) Artemidorus gets close enough to Cæsar to deliver his letter and asks him to read the scroll ("schedule") he offers. Decius edges Artemidorus away and begs Cæsar to read at his leisure a petition from Trebonius, which he presents. Artemidorus anxiously implores Cæsar to read his petition first because, he says, it touches Cæsar more closely than the other. Cæsar replies, with dignity, that what touches him personally shall be provided for, or attended to, last. The *Arden* editors find that this line has "the true imperial ring". Artemidorus implores Cæsar not to delay the reading and Cæsar questions his sanity. Publius edges the man out of the way and Cassius rebukes him for urging a petition in the street.

As the senators are going into the House, or taking their place on the stage, buzzing conversations are going on. Popilius Lena says to Cassius that he hopes his enterprise may thrive and Cassius inquires, 'What enterprise?' But Popilius leaves him and goes toward Cæsar. Brutus asks what Popilius has said and Cassius gives the information, adding that he fears the plot has been discovered. Brutus' eye follows Popilius and he advises Cassius to watch, too. But Cassius turns to speak to Casca and tells him to be prompt in carrying out his part (which is to strike the first blow), because they fear some obstruction of their plans. He turns to Brutus nervously and asks what they can do, convinced that Popilius is warning Cæsar and perhaps heading a counter-plot. If their scheme becomes known, he says, Cassius will never turn his back to Cæsar in defeat, but will kill himself. This reading of the line is based on Malone's substitution of the word "on" for "or"—"Cassius 'on' Cæsar". Others interpret "turn back" to mean "return to his home." Brutus has kept his eyes on Popilius and now begs Cassius to keep steady, assuring him that Popilius is not speaking of their plans because he is smiling and Cæsar's color does not change. Cassius sees that Trebonius is taking Mark Antony out of the chamber, according to plans, and mentions it to Brutus. Decius, too, is alert to see if all the plans are working out and asks where Metellus Cimber is. Metellus must play his part now, Decius urges, and go to Cæsar with his petition. Brutus, apparently the calmest of them all, says Metellus is ready ("addressed"), and directs the others to press near and be prepared to second the suit that will be presented. Cinna speaks aside to Casca and reminds him that he is to be the first to strike Cæsar. Is Brutus' calmness traceable only to his own character, or is it to be found largely in his attitude toward the cause? Is his the least personal attitude?

Cæsar calls the meeting to order informally by asking if they are ready for the business of the day. *The New Clarendon* edition notes that "the words in their setting suggest another meaning to the audience". What is amiss, the speaker then asks, that Cæsar and his Senate must redress? On the phrase "Cæsar and his Senate" the *Arden* edition comments, "The fact that the Senate was Cæsar's instrument was not so galling to the bookish republicans like Brutus as his assuming that it was so, just as it was the idea of the coronation that shocked them rather than the actual power. Cæsar's phrase is an apt spur to hesitation on their part." Professor Kittredge observes on the phrase, "The royal airs which Cæsar gives himself in this scene, though not in accordance with his historical character, have dramatic propriety. Their purpose is to justify the act of the conspirators which, if our sympathies are not on their side, will appear to be cowardly assassination."

Metellus kneels before Cæsar and in obsequious terms pretends to throw his humble heart at his feet. Cæsar protests against the action and says these bowings and lowly curt'sies might move the feelings of ordinary men and turn "what is predestined and decreed from the beginning into laws as subject to change as children's rules; that is, 'they are as likely to do that as to affect me, because I am not an ordinary man'." This reading is from the *Arden Shakespeare*. Mason prefers to read the word "play" in place of "law", making the sentence mean: making things that are predestined into mere child's play. Cæsar asks Metellus not to be foolish ("fond") enough to think that Cæsar bears such a fickle or inconstant disposition ("rebel blood") that it can be melted or dissolved from its original quality of firmness with the things that melt fools, namely sweet words, curt'sies made with the knee bent low, and base, spaniel-like fawning. Your brother is banished by decree, he says emphatically to Metellus. *The New Clarendon* Shakespeare says, "Cæsar speaks of his acts, such as the banishment of Cimber, as if they were the laws of the Medes and Persians." If Metellus, the speaker goes on, continues to bend and pray and fawn for his brother, Cæsar will spurn him out of his way as he would a common cur. The suppliant must know, the great man declares, that Cæsar does not do wrong nor will he, in the matter at hand, be otherwise convinced or unsettled ("satisfied") without sufficient proof ("cause"). Most of the critics find this one of Cæsar's "grandiloquent" speeches. One editor [3] says, "Cæsar's arrogance of speech and manner, the insults he heaps upon the petitioners, in serene unconsciousness that he is either insulting or arrogant—these things go far to excuse the flattering hypocrisy of the conspirators, which otherwise would disgust us with them and with their whole design. Brutus, we feel, was right in fearing that the crown would change Cæsar's nature." After studying this and similar comments, the student has the right (and this right would be most generously granted him by the critics themselves) to consider whether Shakespeare is not keeping closer to his history than is supposed and that he is making Cæsar say here that the order is changing in Rome now that the head of the government is no longer to be won over to this cause or that by base, spaniel fawning. The student may well keep in mind, too, the thought of the author quoted above that Cæsar, the individual, is "serenely unconscious that he is either insulting or arrogant."

Metellus asks if there is no voice more worthy than his own that will sound more sweetly in great Cæsar's ear in urging the recall of his brother. Whether it is

[3] Kittredge.

prearranged or whether Brutus recognizes himself as the one most worthy to make the plea, he kneels and kisses the hand of Cæsar, telling him that it is not in flattery but to ask as a personal favor that Publius Cimber may have his freedom by the repeal of the banishment. "When Brutus stoops in the guise of a petitioner, we cannot suppose it is merely with treacherous adroitness:

'I kiss thy hand, but not in flattery, Cæsar'.

Knowing the man, do we not feel that this is the last tender farewell?" [4] Cæsar is surprised to find Brutus adding his voice to this attempt to move him from his purpose. Cassius kneels, begging Cæsar's pardon for his presumption but calling attention to the fact that he is kneeling as low as Cæsar's feet in his plea for Publius Cimber. A critic [5] finds that "No grounds of right are given by either side for asking or granting the pardon of Publius Cimber; the request is hardly meant in earnest by the conspirators, who are simply seeking an opportunity for carrying out the assassination. Hence Cæsar may be held justified in his refusal; he may be regarded as the embodiment of law, which cannot yield to mere feeling."

Cæsar speaks at length. He tells them that he could very likely ("well") be moved easily if he were like they are—in being willing to move others from their purpose, for then he would be the sort of man

[4] MacCallum.　　　　　　　[5] Snider.

to be moved by prayers. He is constant as the northern star, he affirms, the star that is so firmly fixed
and of such undisturbable nature that it has no equal
in the firmament. The skies are adorned with un-
numbered stars ("sparks"), he goes on, and they all
shine with burning fire, but there is only one that
holds a fixed place. So it is in this world that is
adorned with, or inhabited by, men. These men are
flesh and blood and "apprehensive." According to
Mason, "apprehensive" does not here mean "suscep-
tible of fear" but "intelligent" or "capable of appre-
hending". They are intelligent men, Cæsar is telling
them, then, but among all their number he knows
only one that holds his position so firmly that he is
unshaken by disturbances about him. This one man
is himself, he declares, and he begs them to permit
him to show this firmness a little in the matter before
them. He was confident and firm in purpose in ban-
ishing Cimber and wishes to remain constant. Cinna
begins to plead, but is interrupted and bidden to go
hence. Then Cæsar asks if they would lift up Olympus. This sentence is generally thought to mean that
Cæsar is comparing himself with Mount Olympus.
We may challenge that reading, even though it has
long been accepted, when we recall that the Elizabethans were more familiar with their Homer than
we are and with the literature that grew out of the
Homeric stories. They were accustomed to think of
the Fates

"to whom the heathens yield all power
Whose dooms are writ in marble to endure," [6]

and they knew that those Fates had divided Heaven, Sea, and Hell between the three sons of Saturn. Jupiter drew Olympus, or Heaven, Neptune the Sea, and Pluto Hell. The Elizabethan audience, then, may have understood this line to mean, Will you disturb the stronghold of Jupiter himself? Will you interfere in the domain of the highest gods, and meddle with the decrees of fate? Cæsar's faith in his own place in the destiny of the world was well known. Decius is still conceited enough to think that he can break down Cæsar's decision, but he is repelled and asked if Marcus Brutus himself has not knelt before Cæsar in vain.

Most of the critics find arrogance, self-laudation, and the pride that is said to go before a fall in the foregoing speech. If we consider the historical Cæsar, whose life Shakespeare knew and greatly admired, and couple that consideration with our knowledge of the Elizabethan theatre which permitted a character to explain himself, we might reasonably contend that it was the dramatist's intention to present Cæsar as a person who was, in truth, as constant as the northern star, basing his characterization on the theory that, during the hundreds of nights he had spent lying out in the open, Cæsar had held the northern star before himself as an ideal, and had trained his mind to think of himself as a constant person. However, no un-

[6] *The Golden Age*—Thomas Heywood.

biased commentator will insist upon or stress a theory without presenting for fair-minded scrutiny the interpretations of outstanding critics. Some of these interpretations will be quoted at the close of Act III.

Casca stabs Cæsar from behind; then the others follow. Last of all, Brutus uses his sword. Before he falls, Cæsar utters the now familiar cry, "Et tu, Brute!" (And you, Brutus!) When we have reviewed the life of Julius Cæsar in the light of its highest nobility, this line takes on a little different meaning than the one usually accepted—a greater and deeper significance. The usual interpretation is, Have you, Brutus, joined with these men who wish to kill me? Great as was his love for Brutus, Cæsar had long lived above the plane where personal contacts count for enough to break the spirit. Surely the line must mean, then, And have you, too, Brutus, failed to understand? If there is no understanding even where he counted on it most, his thought concludes, then the struggle is over. In this failure to find understanding of his high ideals for Rome and appreciation of the task he had undertaken seems to lie the tragedy of Julius Cæsar—not in his assassination. A biographer [7] gives this brief description of the end: "He looked around, and seeing not one friendly face, but only a ring of daggers pointing at him, he drew his gown over his head, gathered the folds about him that he might fall decently and sank down without uttering another word."

[7] Froude.

Cinna is the first to remember the program, and he cries, "Liberty! Freedom! Tyranny is dead!" He reminds the others that they are to go with their proclamation into the streets. Cassius attempts to assume leadership again, but is somewhat indefinite in his instructions that some of them go into the common pulpits. (These were rostra in the market-place.) He ends with the planned battle-cry, "Liberty, Freedom, Enfranchisement!" Brutus, keeping calm with apparent effort, begs the people and the senators not to be frightened, not to flee in terror, but to remain where they are. He assures them that ambition's debt is paid, meaning that Cæsar has paid for his ambition. Casca urges Brutus to go to the pulpit and explain the assassination, and Decius adds the request that Cassius, too, address the people. But both leaders are too much confused to comply with these requests, and Brutus rather unaccountably remembers Publius. Cinna says Publius is quite confounded with the uproar. Metellus Cimber is nervous enough to be afraid that some friend of Cæsar may retaliate, and he urges the assassins[8] to stand together. Brutus rejects his suggestion and denies the necessity of standing on the defensive. He speaks to Publius, assuring him that no harm is intended to him or anyone; then asks him to help spread the message. But Cassius' consideration is more practical and kindly, for he urges the old man to get away from the crowd that is assembling, lest his feeble strength be crushed,

[8] The word "conspirator" has become "assassin".

or some other harm come to him. Brutus then seconds Cassius' admonition to Publius, and adds that no man must be blamed for the deed except the men who have committed it. It will be remembered that Publius was with the group that called to escort Cæsar and might, therefore, be under suspicion.

Into this confusion Trebonius returns with the news that Antony has fled to his house "amazed" or utterly confounded. Naturally, Antony would not expect the assassins to spare him, and his first thought has been of self-preservation. Trebonius continues his account of the scene outside. Men, women, and children, he says, are startled into dumbness, then they cry out and run as if it were doomsday.

Suddenly a cloud seems to pass over the mind of Brutus, and he addresses the Fates, perhaps not with the thought of asking what their pleasure may be (as some scholars have read the line) but with the conviction that what Destiny has in store will some day be known. Meantime, he adds, we know that we have to die, and it is only the prolonging of life ("the time and drawing days out") that men find important, or of great moment.[9] Casca gives as his opinion of the matter Brutus has touched on that he who cuts off twenty years of life only cuts off so many years of fearing death. Granville Barker finds the foregoing lines of Brutus revealing the speaker at his noblest, "the man of moral courage," but he sees Casca's

___

[9] This same thought occurs, with greater emphasis and significance, in *Macbeth*—this sudden discovery of the prolonging of life immediately after a murder has been committed.

reply as only "savage mockery" which Brutus in his idealism overlooks or cannot comprehend. Brutus replies that, if what Cassius has said is granted, then death is a benefit and they have done a friendly deed to Cæsar by abridging the time that he might have feared death. He admonishes the men about him to stoop with him and bathe their hands in Cæsar's blood up to their elbows, and to besmear their swords. Then, he adds, they will walk forth even into the market-place waving their red weapons above their heads and crying, "Peace, freedom, and liberty!" The modern student must understand the meaning of the word "liberty" as used in Rome. Sir Arthur Quiller-Couch [10] explains it as follows: "When Brutus and the rest talk of liberty, what they meant was the privilege of the old Roman families which still composed the Senate, not the rights of the populace. It was the Senate, not the populace, which resented Cæsar's absolute power." In the next scene of this act, when Brutus speaks to the people of the ignominy and baseness of being bondmen, he is not holding out to them liberty as we know it, but the privilege of being under a so-called "republican" government (which in practice was oligarchical) in preference to being under a dictator. We must know, too, that "A notable Stoic doctrine was that of the universal brotherhood of man, without distinction between Greek and barbarian, freedman and slave, and the consequent duty of universal benevolence

[10] In *Historical Tales from Shakespeare.*

and justice. But in spite of this, Stoicism was in the main the doctrine of detachment and independence of the outer world." [11] The studious Brutus knew all these theories and his thought was strongly influenced by them, but only Julius Cæsar was democratic in his contacts with the people.

Cassius echoes Brutus' request that they stoop and wash over (not necessarily cleanse) their hands. His next sentence is thought by most of the critics to be dramatically false. Why? MacCallum, though finding no truth in this part of the scene, discovers in his study of Cassius that "at the moment of achievement, whatever was mean and sordid in the man is consumed in his prophetic rapture that fires the soul of Brutus and prolongs itself in his response." And Brutus' soul-stirred response is:

> "How many times shall Cæsar bleed in sport
> That now on Pompey's basis lies along
> No worthier than the dust!"

Professor Kittredge throws this additional light on the foregoing speech of Cassius: "Here Cassius seems to predict the writing of the play of *Julius Cæsar*. Modern critics object to the passage on the ground that it calls attention to the unreality of the spectacle which the audience is beholding. To the Elizabethans, no doubt, the contrary seemed to be true: by speaking of plays and acting, the *dramatis personæ* appeared to emphasize the idea that they them-

[11] *Oxford Companion to Classical Literature.*

selves were real and not the players." Cassius adds the thought that in those far distant future ages, when the scene shall be acted over, their little group will be called the men who gave their country liberty.

Decius interrupts the conversation between the two leaders by asking if they are going to carry out their plans to go forth into the market-place. Cassius orders them to set forth, saying that Brutus will lead the way and they will all do honor to ("grace") him by their following him, since they are the boldest and best hearts of Rome.

Antony's servant enters, and is recognized first by Brutus. "The character of the servant's speech," Professor Kittredge tells us, "shows that he was not a menial. He is rather one of those educated slaves whom wealthy Romans employed in the most important and confidential affairs." The servant kneels before Brutus, saying his master has bidden him thus to fall down and while prostrate to say that Brutus is noble, wise, valiant, and honest, that Cæsar was mighty, bold, royal, and loving. He is to say that Antony loves Brutus and honors him, that he feared Cæsar while he honored and loved him. If Brutus will guarantee, or condescend ("vouchsafe") that Antony may safely come to him and be given satisfactory explanation ("resolved") as to the reasons why Cæsar deserved death, then Mark Antony will not love the dead Cæsar so well as the living Brutus; he will follow the fortunes and affairs of the noble Brutus through all the hazards of the new and untried conditions of the commonwealth. One point not to be overlooked in this speech is the fact that, while Antony has instructed his servant to fall prostrate, he has also demanded that Cæsar's death shall be justified.

Until now, as the editors of *The Arden Shakespeare* point out, Brutus has invariably spoken of Antony in terms of contempt, and these editors ask the student to observe "how readily Brutus accepts the honesty of anyone who compliments him judiciously". Whether we accept this reason for the seeming change in Brutus' attitude toward Antony, he now replies to the servant that his master is a wise and valiant Roman and declares that he has never held a worse opinion of him. "Wise" and "valiant," however, make up a somewhat limited list of qualities. The servant is to tell his master, Brutus continues, that, if it please him to come to the Senate-chamber, he shall be satisfied. Brutus then pledges his honor that Antony may depart in safety. The servant says he will fetch Antony, and goes out. Brutus remarks confidently that he knows they will have Antony for a good friend, but Cassius is doubtful. Cassius wishes they may have the friendship, but he has a presentiment ("mind") that fears Antony a great deal. And, he adds, his misgivings always turn out very much to the point, or prove unpleasantly near the truth. Kittredge tells us that *shrewdly* means "plaguily" or "confoundedly" and has not the modern sense of "acutely." "It was, however," he adds, "perfectly dignified, and not, like the modern equivalent, colloquial."

Antony enters.[12] He ignores, or does not hear, the welcome of Brutus; he ignores, or does not see, the other assassins. He walks to the foot of Pompey's statue where the body lies. Perhaps it had never occurred to him that Cæsar was not a large man, for now his first thought is of the smallness of the inert form. In the deep voice that must have belonged to his breadth of chest he says:

> "O mighty Cæsar! dost thou lie so low?
> Are all thy conquests, glories, triumphs, spoils,
> Shrunk to this little measure?"

These words are too pregnant with feeling to permit any sort of comment. They echo in the heart and mind of the sympathetic reader as do no other lines of the play, and find a solemn response there. This is our first view of the serious side of Mark Antony. We have seen him only as a gamester, though, to be sure, we have glimpsed his devotion to Cæsar. Do we not also see him here as a brave man, unafraid to show his love for Cæsar in the presence of the assassins?

Antony bids a solemn farewell to Cæsar, then turns slowly to the others. He does not know, he says, what the gentlemen intend, who else must shed his

---

[12] This passage from G. Wilson Knight's *Principles of Shakespearean Production* is of interest here. "Each part of the stage has its own significance. Exits, for example, should not be chancy things. Within a scene one side of the stage may quickly get charged with a certain association. You can spoil Antony's entrance after Cæsar's murder by making him come in by a conspirator-impregnated side."

blood or who else has overgrown his power. As for himself, there is no hour so fit to die as Cæsar's death hour and no instrument so worthy to be used for such a deed as the swords that are made rich with the most noble blood of all this world. He beseeches them, if they have a grudge against him ("bear me hard"), that they fulfill their pleasure with him while their purpled hands are still reeking and smoking. If he should live a thousand years, he could never find himself so ready ("apt") to die; no place would please him so much as here by Cæsar, and no means of death be so welcome as to be cut off by the choice and master spirits of the age. The student should watch Antony's speeches carefully to detect sincerity or insincerity. He must consider, too, whether Antony is already beginning to make plans. Is he being perfectly frank here, or is he biding his time and disarming suspicion? Has he had time to make plans? Was there greater necessity for alertness and quickness in finding means of self-protection in earlier times? Brutus implores Antony not to beg his death of them and explains, almost apologizes. Though they must appear bloody and cruel, he says, as is indicated by their hands and their present act which Antony can see, yet he sees only their hands and the bleeding business they have done. He does not see their hearts which are full of pity, pity to the general wrongs of Rome. And this pity for Rome has done this deed on Cæsar, pity driving out pity as fire drives out fire. As to Antony, their swords have leaden points. In

the next sentence the words "in strength" offer difficulties. Mason, very reasonably, would read in their
place "exempt". This would clear the meaning quite
acceptably. *The New Clarendon Shakespeare* says,
"If the reading of the Folio is right it ['in strength
of malice'] must mean 'with a close grasp such as
that only common in grappling with a foe'." Kittredge reads the sentence, "Our arms, violent in enmity as they seem, and our hearts, which cherish
brotherly feelings toward you, receive you in. Malice
means simply 'enmity'." *The Arden Shakespeare* has
this note on the sentence: "Brutus means that toward him they have no more malice than brothers
have toward one another." They receive Antony,
Brutus concludes, with all kind love, good thoughts,
and reverence.

The practical Cassius now promises Antony that
his voice shall be as strong as any in disposing of new
dignities. The comment of Mark Hunter on this
speech should not be overlooked: "It is significant
that Brutus, so scrupulous not to stain the honesty of
the cause by the imposition of an oath, should suffer
such an utterance as this of Cassius to pass without
protest, and with apparent approval. He either cannot or will not see the true character of his associates,
and the punishment which waits on blindness, at once
intellectual and moral, is at hand." The student will
do well to keep in mind this thought of Brutus' moral
blindness, to be considered and carefully weighed as
the play unfolds. Brutus tells Antony that if he will

but wait until they have appeased the multitude, who are beside themselves with fear, they will report ("deliver") to him the reasons why he, Brutus, who loved Cæsar when he struck him, has proceeded in this way. Is this a suggestion that only his own action needs explanation? Is there evidence of an exaggerated ego here, or do we sense the beginning of some "rationalization"? Is Brutus still convinced that the other conspirators were moved by the same considerations as he, or is he beginning to see that he was alone in his idealism?

Antony says he does not doubt their wisdom and asks them to extend to him their bloody hands. He shakes hands with them in turn: Brutus, Cassius, Decius Brutus, Metellus, Cinna, Casca, and Trebonius. The student will need to decide whether he is hypocritical here. He himself exclaims that, alas, he does not know what explanation he must make to them for his action. His reputation ("credit") now stands on such slippery ground that they must regard ("conceit") him in one of two bad ways: either he is a coward, afraid to oppose them, or he is insincere in approving their action. He turns to the body of Cæsar and addresses the man he has known, declaring that it is true that he loved him. If Cæsar's spirit is looking down upon them now, he says, shall it not grieve him even more keenly than his death to see his Antony making peace with his foes and shaking their bloody fingers in the very presence of his corpse. The words "Most noble" are addressed to Cæsar and are equivalent to "most noble one". If Antony had as many eyes as Cæsar has wounds, the speaker goes on, and these eyes were weeping as fast as the blood has streamed from the wounds, it would be more becoming to him than to unite ("close") in terms of friendship with his enemies. He begs pardon of Julius, saying that here the brave hart was brought to bay and here fell; here his hunters stand marked with the signs of his destruction ("signed in thy spoil") and crimsoned in his death, or crimsoned in the stream ("Lethe") which bears him to oblivion. He addresses the world, saying it was the forest in which this hart roamed, and this hart was the heart of the world.[13] As if carried away by his own imagery, Antony exclaims, How like a deer thou dost lie, hunted down by many princes. Is there any question as to the genuineness of Antony's feelings here? Reading the speech over from the line, "That I did love thee, Cæsar, O, 'tis true" do we not find him gradually forgetting his surroundings in the intensity of his feelings for the murdered Cæsar and speaking more and more out of a sorrowing heart? Though opinions of Antony's character may vary, the genuineness of his love for Cæsar is not often questioned.[14] Do we not glimpse a moving

[13] The Elizabethans found it difficult to resist the temptation of a pun, even in serious moments.

[14] As to the historical Antony's knowledge of the conspiracy, the more reliable writers are of the opinion that Trebonius may have sounded him out as a possible member of the "faction". These historians blame Antony only for not revealing the plot. But, surely, it must have seemed incredible to him that it would be carried out.

tenderness of feeling in his picture of the fallen deer? Many times in the forests of Gaul he had seen these animals hunted down. Is it not fitting that Antony should take his illustration from a familiar, homely event?

Cassius approaches Antony and breaks into his thought by calling his name. Antony seems to take the interruption as a reprimand—unless he is acting to some extent, as some think. He urges that even the enemies of Cæsar will say that Cæsar was like a deer pursued by hunters and adds that in a friend it is calm, moderate praise. Cassius briefly denies any intention of blaming Antony for praising Cæsar, and asks bluntly what agreement Antony intends to make with them. More pointedly he wants to know if Antony will be marked down on their list ("pricked") and counted among the friends of the assassins. Or, he demands, shall they go on and not depend on Antony? Antony answers that it was to make himself one of them that he took their hands, but that his thought was deflected when he looked down on Cæsar. He declares his friendship and love for all of them *upon this hope,* or *with this expectation,* that they will give him reasons why and wherein Cæsar was dangerous. The fact should not be overlooked here that Antony makes a reservation in his proffer of friendship.

Brutus takes up the challenge and declares that, if it were otherwise (if Cæsar were not dangerous), this would then be a savage spectacle. Their reasons, he assures Antony, are so full of good intentions that, even if Antony were Cæsar's son, he would be satisfied. Antony expresses himself as seeking nothing more in the way of satisfaction. He then makes the request, calling himself a "suitor", or petitioner, that he may show Cæsar's body in the market-place and himself speak from the pulpit during the funeral ceremonies, as becomes a friend.

Brutus grants the permission at once. Cassius interposes and draws Brutus aside to warn him that he does not realize what he is doing. He begs Brutus not to give his consent to Antony's request, and asks in alarm if Brutus does not know how much the people may be moved by what Antony may say. But Brutus seems bent on being generous to Antony and, begging the pardon of Cassius, announces his intention of going into the pulpit first and showing the reasons for Cæsar's death, referring to the dead man as "our Cæsar." Whatever Antony shall say, he argues, he will declare is spoken by permission of their group and because they are willing ("contented") that Cæsar shall have all true rights and careful ceremonies. This procedure will do them more good than harm, he continues. Commenting on this speech and Brutus' attitude, MacCallum says, "The infatuation is almost incredible, and it springs not only from generosity to Antony and Cæsar but from a fatal assumption of the justice of his cause, and the Quixotic exaltation the assumption brings with it. For if it were ever so just, could this be brought home to the Roman people?" Cassius yields to Brutus once more, but declares that he does not like the plan and doubts the result. One of the commentators goes so far as to say that in these differences of opinion Cassius is always right. Brutus tells Antony to take charge of the body, then gives some instructions about what he shall or shall not say in his funeral oration. Antony may speak all the good he can think of or invent ("devise") of Cæsar, and he must say that he does it by permission of the group, otherwise he shall be permitted no part in the funeral ceremonies. It shall be understood, also, that Antony is to speak from the same pulpit as Brutus, and after Brutus' speech is ended. Antony agrees and says, with seeming humility, that he desires no more. The assassins go out and Antony is left alone. Commenting on the foregoing part of the scene, Sir John Squire says, "There is a slight awkwardness of construction in *Julius Cæsar* where Brutus and his friends, with Antony who has entered, are for so long left alone with Cæsar's body, none of those who fled returning—and this before the Capitol of Rome."

Antony, standing alone beside the body of Cæsar, pours out his heart in a torrent of words addressed to the dead man. He begins by begging pardon of the bleeding piece of earth for being gentle with his butchers. Then he says *with no one about to hear and no one to be influenced or impressed,*

> "Thou art the ruins of the noblest man
> That ever lived in the tide of times."

The "tide of times" is generally taken to mean the course of the ages. However, in *The Shakespeare Society Papers* we find the suggested substitution of "tides" for "tide." The writer continues, "Tides" [is] a Saxon word for epochs, eras, annals but commonly the last. . . . I ask all the critics where is the similarity of Tide and Time? One flows without ebbing, the other ebbs as often as it flows." Antony must be saying, then, that Cæsar was the noblest man that ever lived in the annals of time. He calls woe to the hand that has shed this precious blood, then makes a prophecy in the presence of the wounds which he describes as "dumb", but which he imagines vainly opening ruby lips as if to beg his voice and the expression of his tongue. And this is the terrible prophecy:

> "A curse shall light upon the limbs of men;
> Domestic fury and fierce civil strife
> Shall cumber all the parts of Italy;
> Blood and destruction shall be so in use,
> And dreadful objects so familiar,
> That mothers shall but smile when they behold
> Their infants quartered with the hands of war."

Having given this picture of the curse that shall come upon men,[15] of the domestic fury and civil strife that shall oppress and strangle all normal activities in every part of Italy, until blood and destruction and dreadful sights [16] shall become so familiar that moth-

---

[15] The word "lives" has been substituted for "limbs" by some editors. See *Furness Variorum* for detailed discussion.

[16] See "object", O.E.D. and *Onions' Glossary.*

ers can look on and smile when their babes are cut to pieces, and all pity shall be choked because cruel deeds have become so common, he pictures Cæsar's spirit roaming about like a wild beast seeking prey, with Ate, the Greek goddess of strife and ruin by his side, having come hot from hell. And this wandering, vengeful spirit shall cry, "Havoc" or "No quarter", thus giving an order for pillaging and merciless slaughter. This is the commonly accepted interpretation of the word "havoc" but in *The Shakespeare Society Papers* we find the following emendation and interesting information: "I should request to know what idea *Havock* represents? to me none: to make this quite clear, *vide* the Book of Sports, or *Laws of the Paddock,* published the 2nd of King James I, where are these directions: 'No Keeper shall *slip* his Greyhound till the Warden throws down his Wardour and cries, "Hay! voux!"' Undoubtedly, then, the text is Hay! voux! At that time Horseracing, as now practiced, was unknown, and all races were Dog to Dog . . . Hay! voux! is Dog Language to this day with Harriers." [1844] So, according to this interpretation, Antony is saying the dogs of war shall be unleashed by the spirit of Cæsar acting as warder and crying in a monarch's voice, Hay! voux! These "dogs of war" are named in Henry V [17] as *Famine, Sword* and *Fire.* All this, Antony says, shall Cæsar's spirit do in order that this foul deed shall smell to heaven as will the stinking

[17] Prologue to Act I.

corpses which shall seem to be groaning to be buried.

A servant enters and Antony recognizes him as belonging to Octavius. Antony recalls that Cæsar had written to this young nephew to come to Rome.[18] The servant says Octavius received the letter and is coming. He begins to deliver his message and then stops and exclaims as he sees the body of Cæsar. Antony notes that his heart is swelling with grief and bids him go apart if he wishes to weep. Then he says the man's grief ("passion") is catching, for he finds his own eyes weeping, seeing the other's tears. He asks if Octavius is coming and is told that he has stopped for the night within seven leagues of Rome. Antony first instructs the servant to speed back and warn Octavius that this mourning and dangerous Rome is no place for him at present; then he changes his mind and decides to have the servant stay until the corpse has been taken to the market-place where he, Antony, will try to discover, by means of his oration, how the people are taking the cruel deed that has resulted from the inhuman nature of these bloody, or blood-thirsty, men. And, according to the way he succeeds, the servant is to report to Octavius. It should be kept in mind during the oration that is to follow that Antony has here admitted the necessity of sounding out the people. Many students find him only cleverly inciting the people. Antony asks the

[18] This is Shakespeare's invention to bring Octavius quickly into the scene. The historical Octavius was at Apollonia in Illyria.

servant to lend a hand and they go out bearing Cæsar's body.

The Elizabethan theatre had no front curtain, and dead bodies had to be carried off at the end of the scene. To effect this removal, different schemes were used. In the case of a distinguished soldier, the problem was easy. An order was given to begin the funeral march with all military honors, and the thing was done. The close of this particular scene was, and is, strikingly effective and pathetically sad in that the remains of the greatest soldier the world has ever known were removed by one faithful friend, with the assistance of a servant.

Shakespeare's characterization has progressed far enough up to this point that the student may now begin to consider some excerpts from critical comments on the leading characters—even though a few points in the passages selected may anticipate later developments.

Granville Barker gives definite classification to Brutus, Cassius, and Antony, then asks the question, "Do not these three sorts of men, the idealist, the egoist, the opportunist, stand with sufficient truth for the sum of the human forces which in any age will be holding the affairs of the world in dispute?" He continues, "These, then, are the three men among whom Shakespeare divides the dramatic realm. The contrast between them, the action and reaction of one upon the other, is most carefully contrived; and by everything they are and do the actors must give it point for on this interchange the play's integrity depends. . . . And this is genius, to choose from the mass the essential and to show the abiding truth in things that pass."

Edward Dowden says of Brutus: "Moral ideas and principles are more to him than concrete realities; he is studious of self-perfection, jealous of the purity of his own character, unwilling that so clean a character should receive even the apparent stain of misconception, or misrepresentation. He is, therefore, as such men are, too much given to explanation of his conduct. Had he lived he would have written an Apology for his life, educing evidence with a calm superiority, to prove that each act of his life proceeded from an honorable motive. Cassius, on the other hand, is by no means studious of moral perfection. He is frankly envious and hates Cæsar. Yet he is not ignoble. Brutus loves him, and the love of Brutus is a patent which establishes a man's nobility. . . . And Cassius has one who will die for him. . . . It is noteworthy that while Cassius thus plays with Brutus and secures him, almost using him as a tool, he is fully conscious of the superiority of Brutus. The very weaknesses of Brutus come from the nobility of his nature. He cannot credit or conceive the base facts of life. He is no instrument by which to gauge the littleness of little souls." Of Antony this author says: "Antony is a man of genius without moral fibre; a nature of a rich, sensitive, pleasure-loving kind; the prey of good impulses and of bad; looking on life as a game, in which he has a distinguished part to play, and playing that part with magnificent grace and skill. He is capable of personal devotion (but not of devotion to an ideal) and has, indeed, a gift for subordination. . . . Antony is not without an æsthetic sense and imagination, though of a somewhat unspiritual kind. He does not judge men by a severe moral code, but he feels in an æsthetic way the grace, the splendor, the piteous interest of the actors in the exciting drama of life."

Sir Edmund K. Chambers says: "In Antony you have a second type of 'efficient' man, none the less efficient, complete and dangerous because he hides his efficiency under a Bacchic mask and a wreath of flowers. Antony is 'gamesome'; he has a quick spirit which loves plays; he

> 'Is given
> To sports, to wildness and much company.'

This deceives Brutus, but it does not deceive Shakespeare. . . . Cassius is not without sparks of greatness in him, but Cassius himself would have been a superman if fate had willed it so. What irks him is not so much that the old civic ideal of freedom and equality should be set at naught, as that he personally should be an underling, and live in awe of such a thing as himself. This is not to say that he is all hypocrite. A complete analysis might disentangle strains of sincerity and of self-seeking strangely interwoven in his composition. . . . Between this Brutus and this Antony a plain issue is set. It is righteousness massed against efficiency and showing itself clearly impotent in the unequal contest. Had we only to do with the fate of individuals, it might pass. But the selection of the artist makes the puppets more than individuals. They stand for spiritual forces, and in the spiritual order the triumph of efficiency over righteousness is tragic stuff."

Moulton says of Antony: "Antony has greatness enough to appreciate the greatness of Cæsar. . . . He is famed as a devotee of the softer studies, but it is not till his patron has fallen that his irresistible strength is put forth. There seems to be one element in Antony that is not selfish: his attachment to Cæsar is genuine." Of Brutus this author says: "Brutus knew his wife better than she knew herself and was right in seeking to withhold the fatal confidence; yet he allowed himself to be persuaded; no man would be swayed by a tender woman unless he had a tender spirit of his own. In all these ways we may trace the extreme gentleness of Brutus. But it is the essence of his character that this softer side is concealed behind an imperturbability of outward demeanor that belongs to his Stoic religion." Of Cassius Moulton says: "Cassius has thus become a professional politician. Politics is his game, and men are counters to be used. Cassius finds satisfaction in finding that even Brutus' honourable metal may be wrought from that it is disposed. . . . He has the politician's low view of human nature. . . . Cassius feels . . . irritation at being utterly unable to find in his old acquaintance any special qualities to explain his elevation."

MacCallum says of Brutus: "However aggressive and overbearing he may appear in certain relations, we never fail to see his essential modesty. If he interferes, as often enough he does, to bow others to his will, it is not because he is self-conceited, but because he is convinced that a particular course is right; and where right is concerned, a man must come forward to enforce it. He is essentially a thinker, a reader, a student." Of Cassius MacCallum says, in brief: "He is not deceived by shows. He looks quite through the deeds of men. He is not taken in by Casca's affectation of rudeness. He is not misled by Antony's apparent frivolity. He is not even dazzled by the glamour of Brutus' virtue, but notes its weak side and does not hesitate to play on it. Still less does Cæsar's prestige subdue his criticism. . . . For there is no doubt that he takes pleasure in detecting the weaknesses of his fellows. He has obvious relish in the thought that if he were Brutus he would not be so cajoled and he finds food for satisfaction in Cæsar's merely physical defects. . . . Yet when all is said and done what a fine figure Cassius is, and how much both of love and respect he can inspire." [19] Antony, this author says, "makes his first appearance as the tool of Cæsar. With Asiatic flattery, as though in the eastern formula, to hear were to obey, he tells his master:

[19] The student may need to wait until the end of the quarrel scene, indeed, the end of the play, to appreciate this last sentence to the full.

"When Cæsar says 'do this' it is performed. He per-
ceives his unspoken desires, his innermost wishes and
offers him a crown. It is no wonder that Brutus
should regard him but a 'limb of Cæsar', or that
Trebonius, considering him a mere time-server,
should prophesy that he will 'live and laugh' here-
after at Cæsar's death. But they are wrong. They
do not recognize either the genuineness of the affection that underlies his ingratiating ways, or the real
genius that underlies his folly. Here, as everywhere,
Cassius' estimate is the correct one. He fears Antony's ingrafted love for Cæsar, and predicts that
they will find him a shrewd contriver. Of the love,
indeed, there can be no question. It is proved not
only in his public utterances, which might be facti-
tious, nor by his deeds which might serve his private
purposes, but by his words when he is alone with his
patron's corpse. . . . It is worth noting the grounds
that Antony in his solitary outburst alleges for his
love of Cæsar. He is moved not by gratitude for
favors past or the expectation of favors to come but
solely by the supreme nobility of the dead."

ACT III—SCENE II

ANCIENT Rome had two civic centers called Fora. One was used as a market-place, and the other for the transaction of public affairs.[1] They were remodelled and rebuilt from time to time by succeeding rulers and emperors. Around the sides of a large, rectangular open space would be found at least one temple for the performance of religious rites, one basilica for judicial functions, and one "porticus" for business purposes. There were also shops and temples built in honor of some god or to the memory of some prominent person. The forum of Julius Cæsar, "Forum Julium", was built on a piece of ground that had cost 100,000,000 sesterces, or about $8,000,000. The dimensions were approximately 500 x 350 feet. One may visualize the size by thinking of 500 feet representing ten fifty-foot city lots. The principal temple was that of Venus Genetrix, the reputed ancestress of the Julii on the paternal side. "Facing the temple was an equestrian statue of the Dictator, the bronze horse of which, supposed to be a reproduction of the famous 'Bucephalus' [Bull-headed steed) had the physical peculiarity of Cæsar's own charger, that of divided hoofs." [2] Also, there were, in this Forum,

---

[1] They had grown out of an early market-place. Shakespeare often uses the word "market-place" instead of "forum".

[2] *The Ancient Monuments of Rome*—Theodore Pignatore.

pulpits of orations. These were always present, though the floor-plan was changed from time to time.

The Romans were earnest students of oratory, getting most of their instruction from Greece. Some years before Cæsar's time three Greek philosophers had come to Rome on a mission to the government. They illustrated different styles of oratory. One spoke "with art and polish", one "with restraint and sobriety", and the third "with vehemence and force". This visit left its mark on systematic thought and orderly composition,[3] and we may find something of its influence in the scene we are about to study.

We go to the Forum Romanum, or the Forum Julium, to attend the funeral of Julius Cæsar. We notice with interest the lavish splendor of the surroundings. Our attention is attracted to the temple of Julius Cæsar, deifying him,[4] and our eyes dwell for a sad moment upon the unfinished temple which the Imperator was building in memory of his daughter, Julia. As we wait, our eyes fall, and we find ourselves studying the great floor-space which is luxuriously paved in colored marbles—much as to-day, at a funeral, we find our attention fixed upon the prismatic colors on the carpet opposite the stained glass windows.

Brutus and Cassius enter, followed by a throng of citizens. There is no herald announcing Cæsar's death, no procession of ancestors of the dead, no mu-

[3] See *Cambridge Ancient History*.
[4] Octavius built another temple to Julius in his own even more magnificent Forum.

sic, and no mourning women singing dirges, as was customary at funerals of the Roman great. (History tells us that Cicero had recommended a private funeral.) The citizens are calling for satisfaction and Brutus asks them to follow him and give him their attention. He tells Cassius to go to another pulpit and take part of the audience with him. He gives directions to the citizens, assuring them that the reasons for Cæsar's death will be given them publicly. The citizens divide, choosing their own speaker, and declare their intention of comparing the reasons given by the two speakers. Cassius goes out with his following and one wonders why Shakespeare chose not to record his speech. Professor Dowden says, "We may be certain that it was fiery, triumphant and effective; we may be certain that he did not, like Brutus, make studious effort to exclude all passion."

Brutus goes into the pulpit and a citizen calls for silence. Brutus asks his audience informally to be patient to the end of his speech. Psychologically, is this a good beginning? Then he addresses them formally as "Romans, countrymen and lovers" ("lovers" having the sense of "friends"). He asks them to hear him for his cause. There still seems to be a stir in the audience and he asks them to be quiet in order that they may hear. Believe me, for mine honor, he continues, and remember that I am an honorable man, in order that you may believe me; judge, or estimate ("censure"), me in your wisdom and arouse your intellectual powers, or keep mentally alert, in order that you may the better judge what I have to say. If there be any dear friend of Cæsar's in the assembly, the speaker goes on, let me say to him that my love for Cæsar is no less than his own. And if that friend should demand why Brutus rose against Cæsar, this is my answer: It is not that I loved Cæsar less but that I loved Rome more. Rather abruptly he asks the question: Would they prefer to have Cæsar living and all die in slavery to a king or have Cæsar dead and all live as free men? Then he makes the assertion that he weeps for the Cæsar who loved him, rejoices that he had some good fortune, "honors him in that he was valiant, but has slain him because he was ambitious." Continuing his balanced phrasing he says, There is tears for his love; joy for his fortune; honor for his valour; and death for his ambition. Can we not visualize him counting off his points on his fingers—one, two, three, four? He goes back to the thought of slavery and asks if anyone here is willing to be a bondman. If there is any such, let him speak; for I have offended him, the orator declares. Who is so barbarous ("rude") that he does not appreciate being a Roman? If there is any such, let him speak; for I have offended him. Who in the audience is so low, or worthless, that he will not love his country? If there is any such, he, too, may speak; for I have offended even him. He pauses for a reply, and the audience disclaims harboring any who wish to be bondmen, any who are not proud of being Roman, or any vile or low enough not to love their country. Brutus replies that then he has offended no one, and adds that he has done no more to Cæsar than they may do to him if he ever offends in the way Cæsar had done. He tells them that the reasons for the killing of Cæsar have been set down ("enrolled") in a record which may be consulted in the public archives. In this record Cæsar's worthiness is recognized and none of his glory lessened; the offenses for which he suffered death have not been emphasized or exaggerated. As the *Arden* edition of the play notes, "the populace was not likely to consult public documents." Would they be discriminating enough to appreciate such a record as Brutus has just described? Brutus was accounted one of the best orators in Rome. Has he added to his reputation in this speech? Does it seem likely that he had ever addressed a popular assembly before?

Moulton says of this oration: "The greatest man in the world has been assassinated; the mob are swaying with fluctuating passions; the subtlest orator of the day [Antony] is at hand to turn those passions into a channel of vengeance for his friend; Brutus, called on amid such surroundings to speak for the conspirators, still maintains the artificial style of carefully balanced sentences such as emotionless rhetoric builds up in the quiet study."

Brander Matthews says: "The contrast between the funeral speeches of Brutus and Mark Antony makes evident Shakespeare's command of both statecraft and stagecraft. Each of them is exactly what that character would then have made; each is excellent in itself, and each reveals at once the strength and weakness of the speaker who makes it. Brutus is a vain man, of large nobility of soul in spite of his conceit; he is an impractical idealist . . . in that he always takes himself too seriously, and in that he lacks the saving sense of humor that springs from an understanding of his fellow man. His address is the work of a trained rhetorician; it is logical and chilly; it is directed to the intellect of his hearers and not to their emotions; it is egotistic, not to call it pedantic; and it displays a complacent ignorance of the psychology of the crowd. It shows that he had failed to profit by his frequent opportunities to understand the temper of his fellow citizens. It is proof positive of his lack of political wisdom and of his unfitness for the part he is playing. He says the things he ought not to have said and leaves unsaid the things he ought to have said."

Edward Dowden comments, in part: "It is characteristic of the idealist that he should treat the Roman crowd—that sensitive, variable, irrational mass—as if it must not be indulged in any manner of persuasion except a calm appeal to reason, and the presentation of an ideal of justice. He begins with a vindication of his own conduct, an apology for Brutus. His manner is deliberate and constrained until he passes from self-defense to a direct appeal to his countrymen's patriotism and love of freedom; and it is noticeable that at this point of his speech, which begins as prose, if not actually verse hovers on the brink of verse."

Granville Barker, after testing out the lines on the stage, has the following to say: "Editor after editor has condemned Brutus' speech as poor and ineffective, and most of them have then proceeded to justify Shakespeare for making it so. It is certainly not meant to be ineffective, for it attains its end in convincing the crowd. Whether, as oratory, it is substantially poor must be to some extent a matter of personal taste. Personally, accepting its form, as one accepts the musical conventions of the fugue, I find it fine, and it stirs me deeply. In many ways I prefer it to Antony's. It wears better. It is very noble prose. But we must, of course, consider it primarily as a part of the setting out of Brutus' character and according to its use and place in the scene. . . . Shakespeare again has been accused of bias against the populace. But is it so? He had no illusions about them. As a popular dramatist he faced their inconstant verdict every day, and for the model of the Roman mob he did not need look further than the audience he was to show it to. . . . A rapping on the desk for 'quiet please' is no way, one would suppose, into the affections of a heady crowd. . . . What he has to say is clear in his mind, but it is not simple, it is tragic paradox. Nevertheless he wins them. . . . He wins . . . not by what he says but by what he is."

Mason, one of the older critics, thus expresses his opinion: "I cannot agree with Warburton that this speech is very fine of its kind. I can see no degree of excellence in it, but think it a very paltry speech for so great a man, on so great an occasion, yet Shakespeare has judiciously adopted in it the style of Brutus—the pointed sentences and the labored brevity which he is said to have affected."

MacCallum tells us that, "even if the cause of the conspirators could be commended to the populace, Brutus is not the man to do it. It is comic and pathetic to hear him reassuring Cassius with the promise to speak first as if he could neutralize in advance the arts of Antony. Compare his oratory with that of his rival. . . . Such a speech would make little impression on an assembly of those who are called educated men, and to convince an audience like the artisans of Rome . . . it is ridiculously inadequate. . . . Nothing could be more neat, accurate and artificial than this euphuistic arrangement of phrase. . . . It is a style unsuitable to, one might almost say incompatible with, genuine passion. . . . It has a noble ring about it because it is sincere, with the reticence and sobriety which the sincere man is careful to observe when he is advocating his own case. But that it is not the sort of thing that the Saviour of his Country, as Brutus thought himself to be, will find fit to sway the mob. Nevertheless, his eloquence was notorious. And this is the man with his formal dialectic and professional oratory . . . who thinks that by a temperate statement of the course which he has seduced his reason to approve, he can prevent the perils of the speech by Cæsar's friend." The student may well pause to ponder over the thought that Brutus has *seduced his reason* to accept the course he has taken—and the writer of this study will request him to keep the thought to the end of the play.

Mark Antony enters with Cæsar's body. It is not only as a friend of Cæsar that Antony bears this important charge. As the surviving consul he was lawfully the highest authority in the state. Brutus calls attention to Antony's entrance and tells the citizens that, though Antony had no hand in Cæsar's death, he shall share in the benefits that will now come to the commonwealth. He tells them that they will all benefit by Cæsar's death. As a parting thought he assures them that, as he slew his best friend for the good of Rome, he has the same dagger for himself when the good of his country shall require his death. The crowd expresses its regard for Brutus by crying that he must live; one suggests that they accompany him to his house in triumph; a second suggests a statue with his ancestors; and a third shouts, "Let him be Cæsar!" Do we not find, then, that, after all, the people wanted a Cæsar? Boas says, "'Cæsar' has developed into a permanent constitutional factor, indestructible by the cancelling of an individual life. It is in effect the proclamation, *Le roi est mort, vive le roi!*" After more of the citizens' talk about honors to Brutus, the speaker begs permission to depart alone. He urges them to stay for his sake to hear Antony, to show due respect to Cæsar's corpse and to honor Antony's speech in which he will praise Cæsar. Permission has been granted Antony to make this speech, he tells them, and he entreats them to permit him to be the only one to leave. He goes out alone, and, as Granville Barker reflects, "We should be made to realize, though he does not, how truly alone." Brandes says, "He is too proud to keep a watch on Antony . . . therefore he leaves the Forum before Antony begins his speech. . . . Many another has acted in this unwise way, proudly reckless of the consequences, moved by the dislike of the magnanimous man for all that savors of base cautiousness." And when he gets back to his study will he think over the cry, "Let him be Cæsar," and still regard the letters thrown in at his window as the voice of Rome?

The crowd urges the "noble Antony" to go into the pulpit. Evidently they enjoy speechmaking and wish to hear more. Perhaps they are flattered. Antony, rather humbly, it would seem, credits Brutus with getting him permission to speak and says he is obliged to his audience. As he is going into the pulpit, there are brief back-and-forth remarks about Brutus and Cæsar. They will hear no harm spoken of Brutus, but Cæsar was a tyrant. Perhaps they have come expecting Brutus to say Cæsar was a tyrant and have been disappointed. Anyway, they are ready to say as much themselves.

Antony begins to address them as kindly ("gentle") Romans, not Romans of gentle blood, but the crowd has not yet been quieted and citizens call for silence.

The speaker waits till they are ready to hear and begins again, this time with a ringing, "Friends, Romans, countrymen, lend me your ears"; and the words not only rang out in the Forum and echoed among the seven hills of Rome, but they have come ringing down the centuries until every schoolboy of sufficient age has felt the thrill of their effect—even though he "hates *Julius Cæsar*." I have come to bury Cæsar, not to praise him, Antony feels his way. The evil that men do seems to live after them, he goes on, but the good is often buried with their bones and never mentioned thereafter. He is willing that this should be true of Cæsar—no praise, no mention of the good he has done. The noble Brutus has told them that Cæsar was ambitious, he goes on. We may be sure he is watching every face now, and that every eye is on him. If that were true, he ventures, it were a grievous fault and Cæsar has paid bitterly for that ambition. *If* Brutus has told them the truth, and *if* Cæsar were ambitious, is what he is saying. They must be wondering what is coming next. Perhaps they are wondering if he is going to challenge what Brutus has told them and say that Cæsar was not ambitious. But he goes calmly on to say that by leave of Brutus and the rest, he has come here to speak at Cæsar's funeral, observing casually and parenthetically that Brutus is an honorable man. Now he speaks of Cæsar. At least he may give a personal viewpoint, he appears to suggest, and he says simply that Cæsar was his friend, a friend who was faithful and just.

It would seem that there could be no objection to this registered on the faces before him, but he weaves back to what he had said before—a statement that has met their approval—that Brutus has said that Cæsar was ambitious. Again he mentions the honor of Brutus. He next dares a little further and reminds them that Cæsar brought many captives home and, when they were ransomed, the money filled the public treasury. There must be a response to this, because it is something they know about; and he asks more boldly whether this seemed ambitious. He tells them that Cæsar wept when the poor were in trouble and comments that ambition should be made of sterner stuff. Again he returns to what Brutus has said and to his assurance to them of Brutus' honor. One wonders if the audience is not divided and whether he is throwing out these backward turning thoughts to appease certain elements devoted to Brutus until they are ready for his next remark. Surely he must find, from some of the faces, encouragement that emboldens him. So he reminds them of the Lupercal when he offered Cæsar a crown, which was refused, and asks if this seemed like ambition. Yet Brutus said he was ambitious, he weaves back again, and Brutus' word is of value because of his honor. Examining the lines carefully, does it not seem that the words, "And sure" raise a question as to the honor of Brutus? Has that doubt appeared before? He is not speaking to disprove what Brutus has told them, he goes on, but is here to speak only what he knows. Then he makes a direct appeal to their affections, reminding them that they once loved Cæsar and not without cause. Why, then, should they not mourn for him, he asks. He turns aside and addresses personified Judgment, regretting that Judgment has fled to brutish beasts while men have lost their reason. Sadly he asks them to bear with him because his heart is in the coffin there with Cæsar. He must pause, he apologizes, till it come back to him. MacCallum says, "We may be sure that whatever had happened to his heart, his ear was intent to catch the murmurs of the crowd." But, as this same author tells us, "We should consider the enormous difficulties of his position. He is speaking under limitations before a hostile audience that will barely give him a hearing and his task is to turn them quite round and make them adore what they hate and hate what they adored." The student must be ready to believe, if he finds it in the lines of the play, that Antony is not the showman he is often thought to be.

The citizens discuss what Antony has said while Antony weeps for Cæsar. They find much reason in what the speaker has said, much wrong done to Cæsar; and they fear that Cæsar's rule will be replaced by something worse. They discuss the refusal of the crown with its proof that Cæsar was not ambitious and threaten that some one will pay dearly ("dear abide") if it be found that Cæsar was not ambitious. They turn to Antony with sympathy, remarking on the redness of his eyes. One says there is not a nobler man in Rome than Antony. Antony begins to speak and they are all attention. Only ycsterday, he reminds them, the word of Cæsar might have stood against the world; and now he lies there so low that the poorest, basest, is too high to be humble enough to do him reverence. This is the thought that struck Antony at the first sight of Cæsar's dead body—the mighty Cæsar brought so low. Perhaps something of that first emotional reaction surges over him, but he controls it and continues, addressing them as "masters," telling them that if he were inclined to stir their hearts and minds to disorder or riot and rage, he would be doing Brutus and Cassius wrong, who, they all know, are honorable men. He will not do them wrong, he declares; he would rather wrong the dead, or himself, or the audience, than to wrong such honorable men. Rather unexpectedly he produces a parchment, Cæsar's will, and says he found it in Cæsar's closet. If the commons could hear the terms of the will, which he has no intention of reading, they would go and kiss dead Cæsar's wounds, and dip their handkerchiefs in his sacred blood, even beg one of his hairs for a memento and, on their death-beds, mention it in their wills, bequeathing it as a precious legacy to their posterity. The people clamor to hear the will, but he bids them be patient, protesting that it is not good for them to know how Cæsar loved them. They are not wood, nor stones, he suggests, but men, and, being men, the hearing of Cæsar's will is sure to inflame them and put them in a frenzy. Then he lets the cat out of the bag (deliberately?) and tells them that they are Cæsar's heirs, warning them again that it is not good for them to know this and declaring that, if he were to give them the details, he does not know what the result might be. Again the people insist that the will be read. Antony asks them to be patient and wait ("stay") awhile. He has gone further than he intended, he apologizes, using a figure from archery. He is afraid he has wronged the honorable men whose daggers have stabbed Cæsar. What is the effect of this oft-repeated mention of honor by this time? What is the effect of this first direct reference to the stabbing of Cæsar? The next line helps to answer the question. A citizen declares the assassins to be "traitors" and scorns the repeated "honorable men." Others take up the cry, clamoring to hear the will and exclaiming against the "villains" and "murderers". Antony pretends to be forced, or finds himself compelled, to read the will—according to our view of the extent to which he is acting. He asks them to make a circle around the corpse and let him show them the author of the will. He asks if he shall descend to the level where the body lies. They urge him to come down. Amid eager commotion Antony descends and they press around him, talking and jostling. He begs them to stand farther off, and officious ones see that he is obeyed.

The citizens are standing back and, to all intents

and purposes, Antony is alone again with the dead body of the man he loved. He stoops and touches the toga, intending to lift it to display the wounds. Suddenly his mind flashes back to a summer's day in the forests of Gaul, when the "stoutest warriors of all the Belgæ," to the number of 120,000, came unexpectedly upon Cæsar's men as they were fortifying their camp. A terrible slaughter of Romans had begun, when one slight man turned the tide of battle; for "had not Cæsar himself taken his shield on his arm, and flying in amongst the barbarous people, made a lane through them that fought before him; and the tenth legion also, seeing him in danger, ran unto him from the top of the hill, where they stood in battle, and broken the ranks of their enemies, there had not a Roman escaped alive that day." [5] For a brief moment Antony sees Labienus alive again leading the famous tenth legion to the aid of their general—Labienus, who was the first to conspire against Cæsar—conspire—conspiracy—conspirators —and now all those conquests, all those glories, all those triumphs are shrunk to this—little—

Antony, struggling with his tears, begins to speak, telling the people that, if they are going to weep, now is the time the tears will come. He touches the robe and says, with a sob in his voice: You all know this mantle. Their minds held a vivid picture of the mantle enveloping and swinging away from the graceful form as its wearer moved with light step

[5] Plutarch.

about the streets of Rome, unattended, when his life was momentarily in danger. Antony begins to tell his audience about the first time he saw Cæsar put the toga on. It was on a summer's evening, that day he overcame the Nervii. That day? The people here in the Forum have reason to remember that day; for, when the news of the victory came to Rome, "the Senate ordained that they should do sacrifice to the gods, and keep feasts and solemn processions fifteen days together without intermission, having never made the like ordinance in Rome for any victory that ever was obtained. Because they saw the danger had been marvelous great, so many natives rising as they did in arms together against him, and, further, the love of the people unto him made his victory much more famous." [6]

Antony shows them the rents in the garment, naming the several assassins whose daggers had made them. When he comes to Brutus, he asks them to note how Cæsar's blood had flowed when the steel was withdrawn, as if it were rushing forth to find if it could be that Brutus had knocked at the door so unkindly. For Brutus, as you know, was Cæsar's angel, he adds. Only the gods are capable of judging, or understanding, how Cæsar loved him. This was the "most unkindest" cut of all. (Elizabethan English permitted the use of double superlatives for emphasis.) [7] When the noble Cæsar saw Brutus stab

[6] Plutarch.

[7] Perhaps we should have retained some of their rules. Emerson once said he envied the schoolboy his double negatives.

him, Antony continues, the ingratitude of Brutus completely overcame him—ingratitude which is stronger than the weapons ("arms") of traitors. Then Cæsar's mighty heart burst, the speaker goes on, and, covering his face, he fell at the base of Pompey's statue, his blood running freely about the pedestal.

"O, what a fall was there, my countrymen!" Antony exclaims, adding that with Cæsar's fall the people present, Antony himself, and, indeed, all the Romans have fallen down, while bloody treason flourished over Rome. The people are weeping now, and Antony observes that they feel the pressure ("dint") of pity. He adds that their tears are precious drops. Are the "kind souls" weeping over Cæsar's sword-rent garment, he asks; then he bids them look at the body itself, wounded by traitors. He lifts the mantle and discloses the slender, still youthful figure clad in its bloody tunic, the girdle still fastened in the unusual manner he had affected in his youth and never discarded. The familiar chaplet has fallen away from the brow it has so long encircled and lies in pathetic futility upon the bier. The people exclaim over the piteous spectacle, the noble Cæsar, the woeful day. One suggests revenge, and they all begin to cry of revenge, of burning, killing, slaying, and with the imprecation that not one of the traitors shall live.

Antony calms the "good friends," the "sweet friends" and says they should not permit him to stir them up to such extravagant, abundant disorder ("flood of mutiny"). What private griefs against Cæsar the assassins may have had that made them do the deed he does not know, he exclaims regretfully. They are wise and honorable and will, no doubt, answer the people with their reasons. The speaker has not come to steal away, or win over, their hearts, he goes on. He is no orator as Brutus is, but, as they all know, a plain, blunt man who loves his friend. All this, he adds, is well known to those who gave him leave to speak publicly of Cæsar. He disclaims having the wit, words, worth, action, utterance or power of speech to stir men's blood. He only speaks right on and tells them what they already know (note the deft little compliment here), shows them sweet Cæsar's wounds that are like poor, poor dumb mouths, and bids them speak for him. But if he were Brutus, and Brutus were Antony, he would stir up their spirits and put a tongue in every wound of Cæsar that should move the very stones of Rome to rise and mutiny. Baring-Gould says, "Antony, who, it must be remembered, was but imperfectly educated, and had never cultivated the art of oratory, had been carried away by his feelings, and by the conviction which his words had stirred among the people."

One of the crowd cries that they will mutiny, and the mob threatens to burn the house of Brutus. But Antony quiets them again and tells them they know not what they are planning to do, because they do not realize why Cæsar deserved their loves. Alas, they know not, he insists. He must tell them, then, and he reminds them of the will. Again they are all eagerness and Antony tells them the terms of the will. To each individual Roman citizen has been bequeathed seventy-five drachmas, about fifteen dollars in our money. They exclaim over the noble, royal Cæsar, and again Antony begs them to hear him patiently. He then tells them that Cæsar has left to them and their heirs forever all his walks, his private arbours, and newly planted orchards, where they may always go for recreation. This discloses the greatness of Cæsar, he declares, and asks when another so great will come. The reply to Antony's question is, "Never, never" from the leader, who then calls the mob to come with him to burn the body of Cæsar in the holy place and set fire to the traitors' houses with burning brands from the funeral pyre. They take up the body and, according to some authorities, seize the furniture from the Basilica Julia to make the fire. As Antony stands alone watching them at their task, he says, perhaps with bitterness, "Now let it work!" Mischief is afoot, he reflects, and he is willing it should take what course it may.

A servant enters, announcing to Antony that Octavius has arrived and that he and Lepidus are at Cæsar's house. Antony says he will join them. Octavius has come as if in answer to his wish. Fortune is in a merry mood, he says, a mood for giving him and his friends anything. The servant delivers the news that

Brutus and Cassius have ridden like madmen through the gates of Rome. Antony replies with unconcealed satisfaction that very likely they have learned how his speech has stirred the people. He asks the servant to conduct him to Octavius, and the scene closes.

We leave the Forum, dry our eyes and, perhaps, begin to think more clearly, remembering that it is easy to become sentimental at a funeral. Searching our knowledge of history, we recall that Calpurnia helped Antony prepare that speech. Together they had planned the reading of the will. Perhaps, then, we admit, the story of Cæsar's donning the toga after the battle with the Nervii was premeditated, too, even fabricated. The story was bound to arouse the mob. That victory had given them a holiday and an emotional debauch that they would long remember. It would be a clever stroke to associate the garment with that event. But would Antony have done almost as well without the reference to the battle? [8]

Turning to the critics we find some brief, quotable comments on the speech which must be read in connection with Shakespeare's lines—not with this interpretation.

Granville Barker says: "One may so analyse the speech throughout and find it a triumph of histrionics. For one thing he writes his part as he goes; and if he can move others, he can equally stimulate himself to action. . . . He can judge his audience to a

---

[8] History tells us that Antony was not even present at the battle with the Nervii; but, after all, we are reading Shakespeare.

nicety. He makes everything easy for them, waits while they think matters over and compare notes and grow readier to listen again. . . . Yes, Antony is the perfect spellbinder, and the simplicity upon which these magicians may presume is apparently unfathomable. This occasion, truly, leaves few tricks left untried. . . . The peroration is masterly on his part and on Shakespeare's. It is a summing up for the mob of every suggestion that has intrigued them; and for us, of every means by which it has been done. We note again the false restraint from passion, the now triumphant mockery of those honourable men, of their wisdom, their good reasons and their private griefs; and again comes the plain blunt man's warning against such oratorical snares as the subtle Brutus set. It is all rounded off with magnificent rhythm, the recurrent thought and word are flung like stones from a sling. . . . We as an audience are apt to join ourselves with the audience in the Forum without further question; it is, indeed, Antony's immediate duty to see that we do."

Brander Matthews says, in part: "Mark Antony's address is a model stump speech. It is swift and fiery; it appeals to imagination and to passion. It is not a mere rhetorical exercise but a masterpiece of persuasion aimed to accomplish a definite purpose. Mark Antony has all the arts of the rhetorician, including that of deprecating his own gifts as an orator in comparison with those of Brutus. The psychology of the crowd that his predecessor ignored or was ignorant of, Mark Antony understands and applies. He is sincere in his affection for his dead friend, yet he uses that very devotion as an element of persuasion. He is cunning, sinuous, resourceful; and he plays on the passions of his hearers, that he may at once avenge Cæsar's death and profit by it. Surpassingly clever the speech is in itself, and intensely dramatic in the use to which Shakespeare puts it."

Richard Moulton finds that "The speech of Antony, with its mastery of every phase of feeling, is a perfect sonata upon the instrument of human emotions. Its opening theme is sympathy with bereavement against which are working, as if in conflict, anticipations of future themes, doubt and compunction. A distinct change of movement comes with the first introduction of what is to be the final subject, the mention of the will. But when this movement has worked from curiosity to impatience, there is a diversion: the mention of the victory over the Nervii turns the emotions in the direction of historic pride, which harmonizes well with the opposite emotions roused as the orator fingers hole after hole in Cæsar's mantle made by the daggers of his false friends, and so leads up to a sudden shock when he uncovers the body itself and displays the popular idol in its bloody defacement. Then the finale begins: the forgotten theme of the will is again started, and from a burst of gratitude the passion quickens and intensifies to rage, to fury, to mutiny."

Sir John Squire is of the opinion that "Probably

no demagogue, from Demosthenes to Cicero, from Cicero to our own day, ever made a speech at once as immediately persuasive and as revelatory of his own character (in this instance both cunning and hearty) as Antony's after Cæsar's death: skillful utterly, truth indistinguishable from falsehood, the thing inspired by the audience indistinguishable from the thing felt from within. But if such a speech was ever made it is only because this speech embodies the concentrated truth about all such speeches: and Antony is exhibited in a few lines better than most orators are exhibited in whole volumes of their sophistical and emotional wind-baggery."

Frederick Boas thus comments on Antony's speech: "He begins with an ironical show of deference to the 'honorable' assassins with the plea that Cæsar was ambitious, and there skillfully glances at incidents which give the lie to such a contention. After a pause, to note the effect of this opening upon his hearers, he introduces a new topic—Cæsar's will, and hints alluring at its munificent provisions. The crowd, wild with excitement, insists that the will shall be read, and Antony, stepping down from the 'pulpit', bids them first make a ring about the corpse of Cæsar, that he may show them their benefactor! It is a superb piece of stage management, paving the way for a final coup—a direct appeal to the emotions of the populace through the eye as well as the ear. He points to Cæsar's mantle, associated with one of his glorious victories in the field, but now gashed and crimsoned by endless strokes, including that 'unkindest cut of all' dealt by 'Cæsar's angel', Brutus. Then, as tears begin to flow from the beholders, he plays his trump card by snatching the covering from the body and displaying it, 'marred with traitors' to the gaze of the throng. The effect is electrical. A confused, hoarse clamor for 'revenge' mounts from a hundred throats, and, in the tumultuous eagerness to hunt down the conspirators, to burn the house of Brutus, the rabble forgets all about the will, which a moment ago it had been clamouring to hear read. No more vivid picture has ever been drawn of the fickle, inflammable temper of the crowd."

Georg Brandes says: "The still more admirable oration of Antony is in the first place remarkable for the calculated difference of style it displays. Here we have no antitheses, no literary elegance, but a vernacular eloquence of the most powerful demagogic type. Antony takes up the thread just where Brutus has dropped it, expressly assures his hearers at the outset that this is to be a speech over Cæsar's bier, but not to his glory, and emphasizes, to the point of monotony, the fact that Brutus and all the other conspirators are all, all honourable men. Then the eloquence gradually works up, subtle and potent in its adroit crescendo, and yet in truth exalted by something which is not subtlety: glowing enthusiasm for Cæsar, scathing indignation against his assassination. The contempt and anger are at first masked, out of consideration for the mood of the populace, which has for the moment been won over by Brutus; then the mask is raised a little, then a little more, and a little more until, with a wild gesture, it is torn off and thrown aside."

Before leaving this scene, it may be well to glance at Cæsar's own description of the battle with the Nervii, only brief portions of which can be given: "The Nervii ran down to the river with such incredible speed that they seemed to be in the woods, the river and close upon us at the same time. And with the same speed they hastened up the hill to our camp, and to those who were employed in the works.

"Cæsar had everything to do at one time: the standard to be displayed, which was the sign when it was necessary to run to arms; the signal to be given by the trumpet; the soldiers to be called off from the works; those who had proceeded some distance, for the purpose of seeking materials for the rampart, to be summoned; the order of battle to be formed; the soldiers to be encouraged; the watch to be given. A great part of these arrangements was prevented by the shortness of time and the sudden approach and charge of the enemy. Under these difficulties two things proved of advantage: (first) the skill and experience of the soldiers, because, having been trained by former engagements, they could suggest to themselves what ought to be done, as conveniently as receive information from others; and (secondly) that Cæsar had forbidden several lieutenants to depart from the works and their respective legions, before the camp was fortified. These, on account of the near approach and the speed of the enemy, did not then wait for any command from Cæsar, but of themselves executed whatever appeared proper. . . .

"In the meantime, the soldiers of the two legions which had been in the rear of the army as a guard for the baggage train, upon the battle being reported to them, quickened their pace and were seen by the enemy on the top of the hill; and Titus Labienus, having gained possession of the camp of the enemy, and observed from the higher ground what was going on in our camp, sent the tenth legion as a relief to our men. , . . . By their arrival so great a change of matters was made, that our men, even those who had fallen down exhausted with wounds, leant on their shields, and renewed the fight. . . . But the enemy in this last hope of safety, displayed such great courage, that when the foremost of them had fallen, the next stood upon them prostrate, and fought from their bodies . . . so that it ought not to be concluded, that men of such great courage had injudiciously dared to pass a very broad river, ascend very high banks, and come up to a very disadvantageous place; since their greatness of spirit had rendered these actions easy, although in themselves very difficult."

Even these brief excerpts give us a glimpse of the generosity with which the writer gave credit to his subordinate officers, to the common soldier, and to the enemy.

Commenting on the Gallic Wars, Geoffrey Parsons[9] assures us that "the whole venture was far more desperate than the calm, lucid Latin of Cæsar's *Commentaries* would lead us to suppose." Then he adds, "A Kipling would have made these barbarous attacks and stubborn defenses of a far-flung battle-line of fighting barbarians in their home lands a thrilling picture."

Another picture, equally as thrilling, and perhaps more inspiring, would have been given us if Francis Parkman might have described the campaigns in Gaul. The theme was one that challenged the highest powers of an historian who was also a philosopher and an artist. "This combination," John Fiske tells us, "is realized only in certain rare types of mind, and there is no more brilliant illustration of it than Parkman's volumes afford us." And again this author tells us, "Many of Parkman's traits of mind and character were distinctly those of a soldier." After quoting from the matchless word pictures in those volumes, this author goes on to say, "When a writer in sentences that are generalizations gives us such pictures as these, one has much to expect from his detailed narrative glowing with sympathy and crowded with incident. In Parkman's books such expectations are never disappointed."

One word picture quoted is as follows: "The French dominion is a memory of the past; and when we evoke its departed shades, they rise upon us in

[9] *The Stream of History.*

strange, romantic guise. Again their ghostly camp-fires seem to burn, and the fitful light is cast around on lord and vassal, and black-robed priest, mingled with wild forms of savage warriors, knit in close fellowship on the same stern errand. . . . Plumed helmets gleamed in the shade of its forests, priestly vestments in the dens and fastnesses of ancient barbarism. Men steeped in antique learning, pale with the close breath of the cloister, here spent the noon and evening of their lives, ruled savage hordes with a mild parental sway, and stood serene before the direst shapes of death. . . . A boundless vision grows upon us; an untamed continent; vast wastes of forest verdure; mountains silent in primeval sleep; river, lake and glimmering pool; wilderness oceans mingling with the sky. Such was the domain which France conquered for civilization." Such, too, was the domain, later called France, which Julius Cæsar conquered for civilization. Only a magician's touch, such as Parkman's, could have spread the panorama of that European wonderland before our eyes and shown us the light gleaming on Roman helmets in the forests of Gaul; only such enchanted wizardry could rekindle the camp-fires of those long gone days and evoke those departed spirits. And if, under the spell of some such magic pen, we could come to know Cæsar's dreams of empire that grew in that soul-expanding new-old world, we might, even to-day, echo Mark Antony's words and say,

"Then I, and you, and all of us fell down."

ACT III—SCENE III

"THIS little scene gives relief in Shakespeare's manner, after the crisis of Cæsar's murder, and also shows how incensed the people are against the murderers, thus explaining the flight of Brutus and Cassius. . . . The first half of the play, Cæsar's murder, thus ends, as it began, with the lawlessness of the mobs." [1] The action takes place on the same day as that of Scene II.

The poet, Gaius Helvetius Cinna, a friend of Cæsar, is shown on the streets of Rome. He is speaking of his dream in which he was feasting with Cæsar. The circumstance unluckily oppresses ("charge") his imagination, he adds. He has no wish to wander forth but something leads him on, he reflects.

A group of angry citizens enters and demands, one after another, to know his name, where he is going, where he lives, and if he is married or single. One citizen demands that he answer each man's question directly, and others add that the answers must be made briefly, wisely, and truly. Cinna answers that he is a bachelor, and a citizen observes that that is equivalent to saying that they are fools who marry, and Cinna will get a bang, or knock, from him for that. He then bids Cinna proceed. Cinna, answer-

[1] *The New Clarendon Shakespeare.*

ing their demands, says he is going to Cæsar's funeral as a friend, that he dwells near the Capitol, and that his name is Cinna. Immediately one suggests that they tear him to pieces as a conspirator. The poor man assures them that he is Cinna the poet, not Cinna the conspirator. They cry, "Tear him for his bad verses!" A citizen says it matters not which Cinna he is, and suggests that they pluck his name out of his heart and send him on his way. Another cries, "Tear him, tear him!" and they go swirling on their way like a pack of dogs, tearing at the helpless poet and crying that they will use firebrands to destroy the houses of Brutus, Cassius, Decius, Casca, Ligarius, and all the conspirators. This is the worst action of the mob, this murdering an innocent man because he bore the same name as one of the conspirators. It is interesting to find that Shakespeare, in all probability, played the part of Cinna. The "Tear him for his bad verses" then brings us a little breath of atmosphere from the Elizabeth stage. According to some of the critics, Shakespeare himself is under suspicion for having "murdered" Cæsar—but more of that soon.

With the close of Act III, we find the titular protagonist of the play murdered and the populace wild in their frenzy against the assassins. Much has been said and written about Shakespeare choosing to kill off his hero in the middle of the play. Some scholars are of the opinion that the play should have been named "Marcus Brutus", since, according to their viewpoint, Shakespeare was more interested in Brutus, or became more interested as his work progressed. Many of the critics contend that Shakespeare has done scant justice to the character of Cæsar, a man whom he greatly admired throughout his life. These things require careful consideration, and the opinions of outstanding critics should be reviewed with the thought of coming to some understanding of Shakespeare's portrayal of the character of Cæsar. In order to accomplish this, the student must put aside, as far as possible, his knowledge of the historicar Cæsar, including the parts of this Study that have been drawn from the pages of history, and study the characterization only as it is presented in the actual lines of the play.

Considering, first, Shakespeare's source material, we find that Plutarch's "Life of Cæsar" is full of inconsistencies. In this account Cæsar is by turns brave and cowardly, noble and ignoble, steadfast and unstable. The Cambridge historians tell us that Shakespeare found in his Plutarch a pathological study in diseased greatness. A comprehensive examination of the play should discover to what extent Shakespeare followed Plutarch too closely.

Turning to the critics, we find M. R. Ridley [2] saying, "Critics have vexed themselves, I think unnecessarily, in the attempt to determine who is the hero

[2] Editor of *The New Temple Shakespeare*.

of *Julius Cæsar*. . . . We expect in the first place
that Cæsar, who gives his name to the play, and is
the most important figure in it, at least historically,
is the hero; but he disappears from the stage half
way through the play, and even while he is on it we
cannot feel him to be the least interesting as the
other tragic heroes are interesting. Nor do attempts
to meet this difficulty by regarding the hero of the
play as something so intangible as 'the spirit of
Cæsar' or 'Cæsarism' carry any conviction. . . . Brutus, on the other hand, is a far more interesting
figure, but apart from the fact that the internal conflict, which we watch with such strained attention in
Hamlet and *Macbeth,* is in Brutus all but over before the play begins, most readers feel that in some
way Brutus never rises to the 'stature' of the great
tragic heroes." This writer finds that the play is a
transitional play, a "bridge" between the chronicles
and the tragedies, but is of the opinion that "it is
idle to quarrel with Shakespeare and distract ourselves from the just appreciation of the play as it
stands, because he did not, at this stage of his dramatic career, conform to the type of drama toward
which he was feeling his way." This author continues further: "There is another odd feature about
this play which is worth a passing mention; that is
the discrepancy, most unusual in Shakespeare, between what is said about the two main figures by
the other characters and the impression which they
themselves produce upon us. Cæsar, as others speak

of him, is the great conqueror and ruler of the world. Cassius, however bitterly he may resent the fact that he bestrides the world like a Colossus, none the less admits the fact; to Antony he is the noblest man that ever lived in the tide of times. But whenever Shakespeare presents him, he not only goes out of his way to stress his physical infirmities, but also puts into his mouth phrase after phrase of the worst kind of egotistical rant, about the northern star, and two lions littered in one day, and so on." By way of explanation of this "rant", this writer puts the question: "Is it perhaps merely that one of the things that at no period of his dramatic career could Shakespeare compass was the inspired rant of Marlowe; that he meant Cæsar to speak in the tones of a great ruler, and made him speak like a Byronic poseur?"

Granville Barker says, after his discussion of other characters, "What now of the giant shadow of Cæsar which glooms over the whole? We may admit that—even while he lives and speaks—it is more shadow than substance. Is the comment too harsh a one that Cæsar is in the play merely to be assassinated? Whether Shakespeare could have done better by him we cannot say; there are plain reasons enough, of course, why it would have meant doing worse by the play. To center every effort (it could hardly be achieved with less) upon a realization of the foremost man of all this world, and then remove him from the action at the beginning of Act III would be to open a gulf which no new interest could fill. But, in any case, *can* a great historic figure be projected on the stage? Shakespeare could but have met with troubles enough in the present attempt. His is above all, at this juncture, a drama of human relationship evolved and expressed in emotional exchange. Now a great man's greatness does not consist of—seldom even exists in—his personal relations. To depict it, then, the dramatist will be thrown back upon description, or narrative, or upon the effect produced in people around. To take the last course may easily transfer our interest to the surroundings themselves; narrative in excess is tiresome, and the great man himself, in person of the actor, is apt to belie sounding descriptions of him. Keep him immobile and taciturn, and the play will halt. If he discourses at length on his own achievements, he will seem a boaster. And if he is always in action we get no picture of the inner man. The convention of Greek drama offers some escape from these dilemmas; for there a man is, so to speak, only symbolically himself, and in a symbol one may sum up a truth. There is refuge in the soliloquy. But, again, Shakespeare, at this phase of his development as a playwright, is using the soliloquy more and more for the disclosure of character by the revelation of thoughts and feelings too intimate for exchange. Such a treatment of Cæsar must have put Brutus in the shade, and he had fixed on Brutus as his hero. He is brought, therefore, to showing us a Cæsar seen rather from Brutus' point of view. A noble figure and eloquent; but beyond this appearance we are not allowed—in Brutus' interests—to penetrate. It is historically possible that the virtue had gone out of Cæsar, that no more was left by now than the façade of a great man. We need not credit Shakespeare with the theory. Dramatic necessity and limitation of form drive him, if he is to show us the minds of Cassius, Brutus and Mark Antony, to let us hear only the sound of Cæsar and see him but as a shadow. But no playwright, finding a character more than he can compass, must ride off on such an excuse. It is obvious that Shakepeare does try, within the limits of his play's safety, to show us the accepted Cæsar of history. His devices for doing so are effective in their kind and the play is saved; and that, surely, is the best that can be said."

Sir John Squire finds *Julius Cæsar* "grossly misnamed," but exclaims, "What a triumph of stagecraft is *Julius Cæsar*!" Then he quotes from Granville Barker as follows: "Butchered by Casca, sacrificed by Brutus—these two doings of the same deed are marked and kept apart—and with no more words about it Cæsar is dead. . . . Yet with the dead Cæsar lying there Shakespeare will continue to give us such fresh interest in the living that, with no belittling of the catastrophe, no damping down nor desecration of our emotions, our minds will be turned forward and not back. This is a great technical achievement." The author quoted (Squire) finds the misnamed play "the tragedy of Brutus the whig" and continues, "the figure stands out though much background is revealed and much ground travelled."

Professor Peter Alexander says, "What is, perhaps, one weakness of the play, the one-sided portrait of the dictator, comes from the need the dramatist felt to emphasize the tendency in the times that had set towards a Cæsar. For though Shakespeare may have had warrant in his source for all the great man's infirmities, yet they are emphasized to show that as far as flesh and blood went, the conspirators had no insuperable antagonist; and that what mocked their daggers was an impersonal power attaching to the man later embodied in the ghost of Cæsar."

E. K. Chambers finds that, "It is perhaps natural that Cæsar should provide the title, as he had done for so many earlier dramas of the Renaissance . . . but it is in Brutus rather than either Cæsar or Antony that the center of emotional interest is found."

Frederick Boas is of the opinion that, "There is a trace of the sublime in his declaration, 'What touches us ourself shall be last served', though it argues an inflated sense of the distance between himself and his fellows. But it is the very intoxication of absolutism that claims to be 'constant as the northern star' or as immovable as Olympus; and the death-blows of the conspirators are a tragically ironical retort to such pretentions of superiority to human weakness." "What is the meaning of all this," Boas continues. "Are we to conclude that Shakespeare deliberately intended to turn Cæsar into a laughing-stock for the benefit of the groundlings in the Globe, or that he had radically misconceived his true character? Is Boswell right when he says, 'There can be no stronger proof of Shakespeare's deficiency in classical knowledge than the boastful language he has put into the mouth of the most accomplished man of antiquity, who was not more admirable for his achievements than for the dignified simplicity with which he has recorded them?' It has been shown, however, that Shakespeare did realize Cæsar's greatness, and he could have had no motive for wilfully misrepresenting him. The fact is that Cæsar is the hero of the play, but not the Cæsar whom we see passing across the stage, weak in bodily presence and will. The result shows that there is something more than mere arrogance in the dictator's conception of himself as a colossal human force. Whatever his personal limitations, he is a transcendent power in the world because he focuses in himself the inevitable tendencies of the times."

Georg Brandes exclaims: "He makes Cæsar a braggart. Cæsar!"

Hudson's opinion on the subject is given as follows: "I have sometimes thought that the policy of the drama may be to represent Cæsar, not as he was indeed, but as he must have appeared to the conspirators; to make us see him as they saw him; in order that they, too, might have fair and equal judgment at our hands, . . . Why, then, may not the

Poet's idea have been so to order things that the full strength of the man should not appear in the play, as it did not in fact, till after his fall? This view, I am apt to think, will both explain and justify the strange disguise—a sort of falsetto greatness—under which Cæsar exhibits himself."

MacCallum says, "It is really Cæsar's presence, his genius, his conception that dominate the story. . . . In the first place Shakespeare makes it abundantly clear that the rule of the single master-mind is the only admissible solution of the problem of the time. . . . He [Shakespeare] reserves his chief enthusiasm for Brutus and never seems to take a full view of Cæsar's greatness in the mass. . . . Again his [Cæsar's] tendency to parade by no means alters the fact that he does possess in an extraordinary degree the intellectual and moral virtues that he would exaggerate in his own eyes and the eyes of others. Independence, resolution, courage, insight must have been his in amplest store or he would not have been able to

> 'Get the start of the majestic world
> And bear the palm alone;'

and there is evidence of them in the play. He is not moved by the deferential prayers of the senators; he does persist in the punishment of Cimber. . . . He neither shrinks nor complains when the fatal moment comes. The impression he makes on the unsophisticated mind, on average audiences and the

elder school of critics, is undoubtedly an heroic one.
It is only minute analysis that discovers his defects,
and though the defects are certainly present and
should be noted, they are far from sufficient to make
the general effect absurd or contemptible. If they
do so, we give them undue importance. . . . Shakespeare can scorn the base degrees by which he
[Cæsar] did ascend. . . . With them Shakespeare
is not concerned, but with plenary inspiration of
Cæsar's life, the inspiration that made him an instrument of Heaven and that was to bring peace and
order to the world. So he passes over the years of
preparation, showing these glories but slightly and
their trespasses not at all. He confines himself to the
time when the summit is reached and the dream fulfilled. Then to his mind begins the tragedy and the
tranfiguration. . . . He represents Cæsar, like every
truly great man, as carried away by his own conception and made a slave to it. What a thing was this
idea of Empire, this 'spirit of Cæsar' of which he as
one of earth's mortal millions was only the organ!
He himself as a human person cannot withhold hom-
age from himself as incarnate *Imperium* . . . and
that is the secret of the strange impression that he
makes. . . . We feel all the more strongly, since we
are forced to the comparison, the shortcomings of the
individual and the splendor of the ideal role he un-
dertakes. And not only that. In this assumption of
the Divine, involving as it does a touch of unreality
and falsehood, he has lost his old surety of vision

and efficiency in act. He tries to rise above himself, and pays the penalty of falling below himself, and rushing on to ruin which a little vulgar shrewdness would have avoided. But the mistake was due to his very greatness, and his greatness encompasses him to the last, when with no futile and undignified struggle he wraps his face in his mantle and accepts the end. . . . The greatness of his genius cannot be fully realized unless the story is carried on to the final triumph at Phillippi, instead of breaking off immediately after his bodily death. . . . Not only then is *Julius Cæsar* the right name for the play, in so far as his imperialist idea dominates the whole, but a very subtle interpretation of the character is given when, as this implies, he is viewed as the exponent of Imperialism. None the less Brutus is the leading personage if we grant precedence in accordance with the interest aroused."

Augustus Ralli,[3] in discussing the work of the above quoted author, MacCallum, calls it "the most through analysis of the play and its characters that has been given to the world." This author continues, "With regard to the much debated character of Cæsar, his failure as an individual has never been better explained; but can we honestly detect the 'idea of Cæsarism' in his unfortunate speeches? Is he not rather living on his former exploits than imagining himself as a symbol? The 'spirit of Cæsar' belongs to the latter part of the play; and—to venture

[3] Author of *A History of Shakespearean Criticism.*

for a moment on burning ground—those who recognize a Marlovian figure in Cæsar and maintain that Shakespeare revised the play might here state their case."

The "burning ground" referred to above has to do, as has been indicated, with the theory that Shakespeare didn't write the play at all, that it is the work of Marlowe, or perhaps Marlowe and Beaumont in collaboration. One full length discussion of the subject is by William Wells, from whose book [4] one brief quotation will be of interest: "Many efforts have been made to explain Shakespeare's 'caricature' of Cæsar. But one might as well beat his brains out to probe the secret of the rainbow under the delusion that it was brushed into the sky by a human painter. There never was a time when Shakespeare could have created such a type unless, like Pistol—Shakespeare's nearest approach to that figure—Cæsar had been meant for comedy. But, reading the play as Marlowe's, Cæsar needs no explanation. He falls naturally into the line with Tamburlaine, the Faustus of the early scenes, the Guise, Gaveston, Barbar—all those vainglorius coxcombs who, after a life of crime and tumult, met with sudden and sanguine deaths. . . . And Brutus owes as much to Beaumont as Cæsar does to Marlowe."

Some further considerations (already touched on at some points in these quotations) which should be of assistance in reaching a better understanding of

[4] *The Authorship of Julius Cæsar.*

Shakespeare's portrayal of the character of Cæsar are as follows:

First: About the time of the writing of this play Shakespeare seems to have been discouraged, almost disheartened, over the limitations of his stage and the materials with which he had to work. In the play which probably preceded this one [5] he had deplored the inadequacy of the stage for representing the "vasty fields of France." And now again he must have found himself chafing under the thought of

> "this unworthy scaffold to bring forth
> So great an object"

as the subject he had chosen. Perhaps, again, he found himself thinking, or saying,

> "O, for a muse of fire that would ascend
> The highest heaven of invention,
> A kingdom for a stage, princes to act
> And monarchs to behold the swelling scene!"

For his task now was to bring upon the stage a man of genius, and even genius itself must quail before the task of depicting genius. To begin with, the stage held no room for the vast stretches of forest that later became France; so any representation of the campaigns in Gaul was out of the question. The same limitations held for Cæsar's extensive travels. The scene must then be confined to Rome. But before leaving Rome, at the age of forty-three, Cæsar had not attained his full character stature, and it may

[5] *Henry V.*

have seemed better to begin the play after his return than to bridge those years of absence and trace the development they had brought.

Second: The educated portion of Shakespeare's audience was familiar with the historical Cæsar and, therefore, needed no full length portrait. Floods of Renaissance literature had brought Roman life clearly before them. Two editions of North's translation of Plutarch had been printed and a third was probably under consideration. Even the habitués of the Eastcheap taverns were familiar (in more ways than one) with the "hook-nosed fellow of Rome." [6]

Third: In approaching the characterization of Cæsar, Shakespeare had two conventions of the theatre available: a character could be built up by means of what others say about him, and, secondly, by what that person says of himself—as well as by what he does. For the revealing comments of major characters he chose three men: the man whom Cæsar loved, the man who loved Cæsar, and the man who envied Cæsar. To the first two he gave significant, outstanding lines—lines that are not given sufficient emphasis by many scholars. The man whom Cæsar loved, who was "Cæsar's angel", said he knew no cause for the assassination except the danger of his becoming ambitious, and in tribute to the great man's character this loved one said he had never known him to be ruled by his own feelings, but that he always reasoned things through. The man who

[6] *Henry IV*, Part II, Act IV, sc. 3, line 45.

loved Cæsar placed his nobility above that of all whose names had been recorded in the annals of time. The man who envied him talked of petty things that had nothing whatever to do with nobility and strength of character or with statesmanship. Unfortunately, the envious one's words have received more attention, not only from other characters in the play, but from many Shakespearean scholars, and even historians.

As to what Shakespeare makes Cæsar say of himself, the lines have been commented on in passing, but a few further thoughts for consideration are: Aside from the theatrical convention which permitted a character to explain himself, the times seemed to require the historical Cæsar to make certain explanations of his stand. In this world that was "sick with a moral plague", where the most brilliant member of the Senate (Cicero) was like a weathervane, it must have been necessary for a constant man to declare himself, particularly when he had been away so many years. In this connection the scholars who have objected to the comparison to the northern star seem to have overlooked, or understressed, the fact that almost with his dying breath he was begging them to permit him to show his constancy a little. Does the student get the impression that Shakespeare himself thought of Cæsar as a constant person? Does he not show the people so dependent upon him that, at his death, they want someone else to be Cæsar? In availing himself of this convention, to what extent has Shakespeare succeeded in showing his audience a man who, in theory or in practice, has overcome all types of fear, physical and religious —in an age that was still trying to extricate itself from fears of the most primitive nature?

Fourth: As to the physical weaknesses, what, actually, have we except his inability to swim as he once had done, his petulance under the tortures of a raging fever, a slight deafness, and Casca's questionable story about the falling-sickness? Shakespeare admits Cæsar's deafness (for which there is no historical evidence) but does he not seem to throw it out merely as a hint that, after all, his physical decline is only beginning? One might even speculate as to its being a temporary after-effect of the fever in Spain, since he has to tell Antony about it.

Fifth: In the matter of Shakespeare's killing off the hero in the middle of the play, it should be remembered that Shakespeare was telling a story—the story of a murder, to an audience that loved a story —and he knew where to begin and where to end a story. As any newspaper man of our time would avouch the first interest of the reading public is in the murdered man and, after the funeral, that interest is somehow transferred to the murderer or murderers. One very simple reply to the critics, who find a dramatic defect in the death of Cæsar in the middle of the play, may be found in the title of the play itself. Shakespeare has not called it "The Life and Death of Julius Cæsar", nor even "Julius Cæsar", which might suggest a life-story, but "The Tragedy of Julius Cæsar". Now the tragedy of Julius Cæsar may be said to have begun when he returned to Rome with a new way of life for his fellow men, only to meet with opposition and misunderstanding, and the tragedy did not end until the murderers were brought to justice and something of Cæsar's ideals were put into effect by Augustus.

Shakespeare has brought Cæsar upon the stage only three times: first, as a leader observing and approving the pastimes and traditions of the people; second, in his home, yielding to the will of his perturbed wife and then reversing his decision (for whatever reason the student may accept) and surrendering to the importunities of the conspirators, and playing the part of the gracious host and true friend; third, in the Senate, where we see him for a few brief moments in the capacity of an executive. Aside from these brief glimpses of his everyday contacts, Shakespeare does not show Cæsar in any serious conversation or exchange of thought with anyone. Is this because there is no exchange of thought possible for him among the men of Rome? How about Brutus? What would we not give for a conversation between Cæsar and Brutus penned by William Shakespeare! Stripped of all the critics' comments, all historical entanglements, all propaganda spread by Cassius, what, then, is the effect of these three views the dramatist has afforded us? Do we not glimpse a lonely, solitary figure? Remembering that Shakespeare, the psychologist, always puts more between the lines of the play than Shakespeare, the dramatist, was able to put into the lines, is it not possible to find that he turned from the insurmountable task of depicting genius and contented himself with painting this illusory personality expressing the deep reflection, born of his own experience, that the truly great must always walk alone,[7] that greatness is often misunderstood because of its human limitations and physical weaknesses, because its daily contacts are not unlike those of other men, if, indeed, those contacts do not become somewhat superficial because of the lack of a common meeting-ground?

Perhaps, too, as has been suggested by some of the critics, Shakespeare was afraid of becoming sentimental about Cæsar. It is very difficult to avoid becoming sentimental about Julius Cæsar.

At this point the student will find it of particular interest to make a careful study of the plate which appears as a frontispiece in this volume. Of this bust Baring-Gould says: "This splendid bust is full of character. . . . There is a wondrous expression of kindliness, sincerity and patient forbearance with the weaknesses of mankind in the face, also a little weariness of the strain of life. The eye is raised, looking far beyond the horizon. This admirable head, in the opinion of Mr. Conrad Dressler, the sculptor, was not done from life . . . it was done by a man who knew Julius Cæsar well, who had seen

[7] Buchan, of the biographers, particularly emphasizes this loneliness.

him over and over again and had been so deeply impressed by his personality that he has given us a better portrait of the man than if he had done it from life. He has caught, and has exaggerated, the peculiarities that struck him—such as the width of the skull. . . . Again from intimate acquaintance with his model, he caught and reproduced those peculiarities of expression which Cæsar's face had when in repose, the sweet, sad, patient smile, the reserve power in the lips and that far-off look into the heavens, as of one searching the unseen and trusting in the Providence that reigned there. . . . The artist forgot the scar—he forgot the baldness in the radiancy of the soul that shone out of that impressive, beautiful face." And, again, this author says, "No face among all the busts that have come to us from the classic epoch is so completely that of the highest and purest ecclestiastical type as that of Cæsar. Put on a biretta and the face is that of an Italian saintly confessor. The lofty arched crown of the head is that of an idealist; it is full of reverence; and that wonderful, far-looking, upward-raising eye, that we see in all the best busts, is that of a man looking away from the world into a region of abstractions, with a strange mixture of longing and sadness. The raised eye is so exceptional, so unique among Roman busts, that it must have been a characteristic of Cæsar."

ACT IV— SCENE I

SHAKESPEARE passes over the confused state of
the Roman world and the enmity and rivalry that
existed between Antony and Octavius during the
period that followed the death of Cæsar. Antony
considered himself to be the logical successor to
Cæsar; but, by the terms of Cæsar's will, Octavius
was made his adopted son and heir and named as
his successor. It has been suggested by historians
that that will would never have seen the light of day
if Antony had known its provisions. Antony played
fast and loose with the fortune of Cæsar in an attempt to establish himself in the position of dictator.
Octavius stood firmly on his rights as Cæsar's heir
and adopted son.

Historically, the events of this scene took place a
year and a half after the assassination of Cæsar.
Shakespeare has condensed the action of the entire
play into five days with intervals. As the scene opens,
we find the rivals together, their differences reconciled, for the time being at least, going over a proscription list with Lepidus. We have our first glimpse
of the twenty year old youth who was to become the
first Roman emperor—a youth whose dreams had
been awakened into fixed ideals by his great uncle's
influence. Also, we are about to meet Mark Antony

with the influence of Julius Cæsar removed. John Buchan's brief picture of Antony as a "magnificent blustering human animal" and of Octavius as a "fastidious youth in delicate health" may help to a visualization of the two. We are introduced to Lepidus, Cæsar's Master of Horse, who has been admitted to a triumvirate principally because he was in command of an army. As has been said, the three are going over a list of political enemies who are to be executed or sent into exile. The action seems to us to be without justification of any kind, even that of political necessity, but in Rome proscription had begun with the wars of Sulla and had come to be accepted as a kind of spoils system. Cæsar, alone, of all the great conquerors, had not been guilty of this practice. One excuse for their action made by the historical Antony and his two associates was that Cæsar's policy of clemency had failed and this was their only course. Such things must be judged, as far as possible, by the standards of their own time.

Antony announces the completion of the list of those who are to die, whose names have been marked down or checked by a pin-prick or some such method. Octavius turns to Lepidus with the information that his brother must die, and asks if this has his consent. Lepidus gives what seems to be a ready consent, but pauses as if he had more to say. Octavius tells Antony to add the name of Lepidus' brother to the list and then Lepidus finishes his sentence. He agrees to his brother's death on condition that Antony's nephew shall share the same fate. Antony agrees, one might almost say lustily, and condemns ("damn") his sister's son with a dot after his name. There is also the thought here of the blot being a stain on the family name. Antony speaks to Lepidus and orders, or requests, him to go to Cæsar's house and bring the will so that they may decide how they can cut off some of the bequests Cæsar has made. We may ask, with the Arden editors, why Antony's proposal to suppress these legacies seems particularly shocking. Lepidus goes on his errand after inquiring where he will find the other two on his return. As soon as he is out of hearing, Antony remarks that he is an insignificant person, fit only for doing errands. Then he asks if this man of so little merit should be one of three to share in their contemplated division of the world and receive a third share. Octavius reminds Antony that he had thought him fit to share with them when he admitted him to the triumvirate. And, he adds, Antony has permitted him a voice in the choice of victims marked for death. Octavius refers to that action as "our black sentence of proscription." Antony reminds the youth that he has had more years of experience than he; then he "puts his cards on the table" so far as Lepidus is concerned. They have put these honors on Lepidus, he admits, only to rid themselves of certain burdens of shame or blame that might be attached to them. And Lepidus will bear his burden of honor, Antony continues, as an ass bears gold. There was an English proverb about an Arcadian ass who "while he carried gold on his back still eats thistles." [1] In Massinger's play, *The City Madame,* we find this passage:

> "Wilt thou being keeper of the cash
> Like the ass that carried dainties, feed of thistles?"

Lepidus may groan or sweat under his burden, Antony goes on, whether he submits to being led or makes it necessary for them to drive him in the direction they would have him go. And when he has accomplished what they have required of him ("brought our treasure where we will") then they will relieve him of all responsibility and turn him off as if he were an ass no longer able to bear a precious load, and leave him to graze and shake his ears—or its human equivalent, which would be to whistle in idleness. Octavius says Antony may have his own way about Lepidus; nevertheless Lepidus is a tried and valiant soldier. Antony poohpoohs the idea and says his horse, too, is that kind of soldier. He, Antony, allots the horse his provender, teaches him his part of the fighting which is to wind, or turn, to stop or run on, every bodily motion of the horse being guided by the rider's spirit. To some extent ("in some taste") Lepidus is like the horse. He must be taught and trained and told when to go. He is a barren-spirited fellow, who is so far behind the times

---

[1] See *Oxford Dictionary of English Proverbs.*

that the objects he wishes to attain, the arts he practices, even the things he imitates, are things that have become stale and out of use for other men. He begins his customs, or practices ("fashion") where others leave off. Antony dismisses the subject by bidding Octavius not to talk of Lepidus except as a piece of property.

Antony changes the subject and gives the latest news. Brutus and Cassius are levying forces to move on Rome and claim their rights as heads of the party. He and Octavius must take immediate action, Antony continues. Therefore they will combine their respective followings in an alliance, call upon their best friends and make sure of them, and stretch all their means to the utmost. The speaker suggests that they go into council to decide how the things they have kept under cover may best be disclosed to their followers and how the imminent perils may be more adequately met. Octavius agrees to all that Antony has suggested. He then compares their position to that of a bear tied to a stake (a figure from the Elizabethan sport of bear-baiting). They are surrounded by many enemies, Octavius concludes, and many who seem friendly are treacherous. Many who smile on them have millions of mischiefs in their hearts, he fears.

This is an outstanding scene as to characterization. Do we find the "noble Antony" of the funeral scenes? What changes, if any, have taken place in him? Do we get the impression that Cæsar has chosen well or ill in naming Octavius as his successor? Will the youth have the fortitude to oppose Antony if such need should arise? Is Octavius optimistic, pessimistic, wary, trusting, strong, weak? Does he know his own mind?

ACT IV—SCENE II

AT THE close of Act III, Scene III, a servant informed Antony that Brutus and Cassius had ridden like madmen through the gates of Rome. Antony succeeded in keeping them out of Rome. In June, following the assassination, he appointed the two to the task of superintending the corn supply from Asia and Sicily. The positions were beneath the dignity of the two men, who still held the office of prætor. They refused the appointments, but thought it best to leave Italy. This decision, or forced move, made them virtually exiles. Later they were assigned to governorships: Cassius to Syria, and Brutus to Macedonia. Before long the two had collected money— tax money from the eastern provinces—sufficient to organize an army. Cicero was paving the way for their return to Rome and to power. At intervals he had also supported the cause of Octavius.

Brutus' army is encamped near Sardis in the southwestern part of Asia Minor. As the scene opens, Brutus is shown standing before his tent with the boy Lucius. Lucilius, one of his officers, enters with soldiers and Brutus orders them to "stand". Lucilius passes the word "ho" along the line to subordinate officers and bids them bring their men to a halt.

Brutus asks Lucilius if Cassius is near at hand and is told that he is already close by and that Pindarus, servant of Cassius, has come with a salutation from his master. Pindarus advances with a deferential greeting and Brutus pays him the compliment that he is a welcome messenger. Then, addressing Pindarus, Brutus goes on to say that Cassius, either through some change that has taken place in him, or by the advice of unprincipled ("ill") officers, has given him substantial ("worthy") cause for wishing some things undone that have been done. It should be noted that this complaint about his friend is made to a servant. To be sure, many servants of the time were superior, educated men. The student may have his opinion of Brutus' action here, and may watch to see if Pindarus is a man worthy of the confidence of Marcus Brutus. But if Cassius is at hand, the speaker continues, he will doubtless be able to explain satisfactorily. Pindarus tells Brutus that he is sure his master will impress him as being just what he is, full of regard for Brutus' wishes and for his own honor. Brutus assures Pindarus that he does not doubt Cassius. Aside to Lucilius he asks how Cassius received him. Lucilius answers that Cassius greeted him with courtesy and proper respect but without the marks ("instances") of intimate friendship, and without the freedom and cordiality in conference that was once characteristic of him.

Brutus sums up the information into a picture of a warm friend whose affection is cooling, and asks

Lucilius to notice that when love, or friendship, begins to sicken and decay, it begins to use an enforced, or strained, ceremony, or formality. There are no such tricks, however, in plain and simple faith, he adds. But hollow men, he goes on, like horses that are hard to rein in ("hot at hand") make a gallant show and promise with their high spirits; but, when the spur needs to be applied, they lower their crests (the upper part of the neck) and like deceitful "jades" (a contemptuous term for "horses") fail to measure up to the emergency. In other words, hollow friends, like mean horses, fail when put to the trial. Is not Brutus almost publicly proclaiming his loss of confidence in Cassius? Is this surprising?

Brutus inquires about Cassius' forces and is told that the entire army is scheduled to encamp at Sardis by night, and that the greater part, including the cavalry, are near at hand with Cassius. Brutus now hears them coming and orders some of his men to march forward quietly to meet them. Cassius enters with his powers and orders are given by both generals for their troops to halt. When the word has been passed along the line, Cassius straightway accuses Brutus of having done him wrong. Brutus exclaims to the gods and implores their judgment. He demands to know, perhaps of the gods and of Cassius, if he is in the habit of wronging his enemies, and then asks if he is likely to wrong his brother. Cassius tells him that his serious, grave [1] demeanor conceals wrongdoing, and when he commits these wrongs— but Brutus interrupts and admonishes Cassius to speak quietly, adding that he knows him well, or, as we might say, can "read him like a book". He advises that they do not quarrel in the presence of their armies, men who should see nothing but love displayed between them, forgetting, perhaps, that only a moment ago he, himself, did not scruple to criticize his friend in the presence of these same men. He asks Cassius to order the troops away and then accompany him to his tent. There Cassius may elaborate his complaints and Brutus will give him a hearing. Cassius gives the order, through Pindarus, for the officers to lead the troops a little farther away, and Brutus gives a similar order through Lucilius. Then he warns the followers to keep away from the tent until he and Cassius have finished their conference. Lucius and Titinius are to stand guard at the door.

This is the first time we have seen Brutus and Cassius since they fled from the indignation of the Roman people. From now to the end of the play the student should be on the alert to find what character changes Shakespeare may have traced, character changes that unfailingly accompany the working out of moral laws. As Professor Lounsbury puts it, Shakespeare "steadily unfolds before our eyes the in-

---

[1] This seems to be the meaning of "sober" rather than "temperate" or "calm"—witness the exclamation and appeal to the gods. However, Professor Kittredge finds self-restraint shown in this speech of Brutus.

evitable results of sin, of crime, of errors of all kinds, even mere errors of judgment. . . . Mistakes of judgment as well as actual sins are subject to the operation of those same inexorable laws . . . those moral laws which control the results of human action."

ACT IV—SCENE III

"THIS admired and admirable scene has sometimes been criticized, even by admirers, as a mere
episode, unnecessary to the plot and not advancing
the action. On the contrary it is as vital an element
in the tragedy as Antony's funeral oration. The dramatic purpose of the quarrel (which is quite historical) is to mark the foreordained downfall of the
conspirators. And this downfall results, as all such
disasters should in tragedy, from both character and
circumstance. . . . Nemesis is upon them. Such is
the dramatic force of this incomparable scene—so
closely linked to every fibre of the tragic development
and tragic action of the piece." [1]

The two generals are alone in the tent and Cassius
starts immediately to explain what he had tried to
say outside. Out there he had begun bluntly to say
that Brutus has done him wrong. Now he explains
that it was because Brutus has condemned and stig-
matized ("noted") Lucius Pella, one of Cassius' most
efficient officers, for taking bribes from the Sar-
dinians, ignoring ("slighting off") Cassius' letter in
which he appealed to Brutus for Pella. Brutus expresses the opinion that Cassius wronged himself in
writing such a letter of intercession, but Cassius re-

[1] Kittredge.

plies that at such a time as this, when national affairs
should be occupying their minds, it is not seemly that
every trivial ("nice") offense should be commented
on. Brutus' "Let me tell you, Cassius" may be read
belligerently or pleadingly. Whichever choice the
student makes must be supported by convincing evidence from other lines in the scene. The words just
quoted are followed by the direct statement that Cassius is severely criticized and condemned for having
an itching palm, or covetous disposition, and that he
is accused of selling and bartering offices to undeserving men. Cassius explodes angrily at the thought
of his having an itching palm. Threateningly he declares that the other knows that he is Brutus, or he
would recognize that, by the gods, this would be the
last speech he would ever make. Brutus replies that
the respectable name that Cassius has borne gives
honor to his corrupt actions and, as a result, the
chastisement that should be his must hide its head
in shame. Cassius' anger permits him only one word
and he exclaims, "Chastisement!" Brutus turns from
the immediate subject, but we see the trend of his
thought as he speaks of the honorable intentions he
himself had, and thought the others had, when they
struck Cæsar down. MacCallum finds his confession
of disillusionment in this speech and says there are
"few more pathetic passages in Shakespeare". Brutus begs Cassius to remember the Ides of March, asking if great Julius did not bleed for justice . Who of
all those who touched Cæsar's body, he asks, was so

villainous as to stab for any reason but justice? Shall one of us, he goes on, that struck the foremost man of all the world because he supported robbers, now contaminate our own fingers with base bribes and sell our widespread reputation for honor in exchange for a handful of money—which, after all, is only so much trash? He would rather be a dog and bay the moon, than such a Roman, he declares. In the garden scene when Brutus was turning over the reasons for killing Cæsar, was there any mention of his supporting robbers? Do we find, then, that Brutus is building up a defense for himself? Do morally healthy people indulge in rationalization? Cassius warns Brutus not to harass him, declaring that he will not endure it. Brutus forgets himself, he goes on, in encroaching on his (Cassius') military rights ("hedge me in"). He is an older soldier, more experienced, and better able to manage military affairs. The argument becomes more heated and, may we say, more petty, as Brutus, instead of recognizing the right of Cassius to stand on his dignity as an elder soldier, flatly and abruptly denies what the other has said. Cassius stands his ground with a brief contradiction of Brutus, and Brutus contradicts him in turn. Cassius moves threateningly toward Brutus and warns him to force ("urge") him no more or he will forget himself. Think of your health, he adds, and tempt me no further. Brutus pushes him away, calling him a "slight man", and Cassius is stunned at the thought of Brutus laying hands on him. He had not thought that possible. Brutus insists on being heard and asks if he must give way to Cassius' rash anger. Cassius is staring at him now in incredulous wonder and Brutus asks if he must be frightened when a madman stares. Cassius calls upon the gods and asks if he must endure all this from Brutus. Defiantly Brutus says he must endure even more of what he has to say. Does the paragraph that now follows express his logical reasons for his stand, or does it contain a succession of personal taunts? Cassius may fret until his proud heart breaks, Brutus begins, he should go and show his slaves how angry ("choleric") he is and make his bondmen tremble. But must he (Brutus) budge? Must he pay attention to Cassius' irritable, touchy mood ("testy humour")? By the gods, he swears, Cassius may swallow the poison of his own ill temper even though it may rend him asunder. From this day forth he will use Cassius for his amusement, yes, for his laughter, when Cassius is hot-headed ("waspish"). Brutus is not a laughing man, and this last statement has a more serious import than if a man like Antony had made it. Cassius can only ask if it has come to this—that Brutus should speak to him in this way. Brutus goes on, asserting that Cassius has claimed to be a better soldier. Then, he adds, prove it, make your boasting true and I shall be well pleased. For my part, he concludes, I shall be glad to learn from such noble men. In spite of what many of the critics say about Cassius being the aggressor in this quarrel, has not

Brutus quite "gone off his head"? Is he not using irritating, taunting, unreasonable sarcasm in place of reason? Cassius defends himself, returning to the assertion he has used before, the statement that Brutus wrongs him. He corrects Brutus' statement and reminds him that he said an elder soldier, not a better one. Then he asks if he really did say "better," apparently willing to admit that he may have misspoken. Cassius had greatly distinguished himself in Parthia, but he seems willing to let that pass. But Brutus answers that he does not care what the other said. Does he seem unwilling to listen to reason? Cassius reminds him that he is moving him beyond anything Cæsar had ever done. Brutus replies that Cassius would not have dared to tempt Cæsar's anger as he has done with him. Cassius flares up at the words "durst not" and Brutus insists that on his life he durst not. Cassius warns him not to presume too much upon his love or he will do something he will be sorry for. Brutus replies that he has already done things he should be sorry for. There is no terror for Brutus in Cassius' threats, he declares, because he is so strongly armed in respectability, or honor gained by his conduct,[2] that threats pass him by as an idle wind which he does not heed. He comes to the point of the argument now and says he sent to Cassius for certain sums of gold which Cassius denied him, adding that he can raise no money by vile means. By heaven, he declares, he would rather make coin of

[2] See obsolete meaning of "honesty" in O.E.D.

his heart and use drops of blood for drachmas than to wring their worthless trash from the hard working hands of peasants by any unjust means. How did he think Cassius was going to get the money, or has that thought not occurred to him? He sent to Cassius for the money to pay his legions, he continues, and Cassius denied him. He inquires if that was done like his old friend Cassius, and continues to ask if he would have given such an answer to Cassius. When Marcus Brutus becomes so covetous, he concludes dramatically, as to lock such worthless ("rascal") coins from his friends, he hopes the gods will be ready with their thunderbolts to dash him to pieces. On this speech MacCallum says, "What does it all come to? That the superfine Brutus will not be guilty of extortion, but Cassius may; and then Brutus will demand his share of the proceeds. All this distress and oppression are his doing, or at least the consequences of his deed, and he would wash his hands of the inevitable consequences."

Cassius denies refusing Brutus the money and again they contradict each other with dids and didn'ts. Cassius says the messenger who returned with his reply to Brutus was a fool. But Brutus' treatment of him seems to have hurt Cassius even more than the accusation about the money, and he says Brutus has broken his heart. A friend, he believes, should bear with a friend's infirmities, but instead of doing this Brutus exaggerates his shortcomings. Brutus says he does not make Cassius' faults greater except when

they are used against him. Examined closely, does
not this sentence seem to suggest that the speaker is
indifferent to the character of others so long as he
himself is not disturbed or inconvenienced? Cassius
concludes that Brutus no longer loves him and Brutus
admits that he dislikes Cassius' faults. Cassius insists
that a true friend does not see faults. Brutus evades
the question by observing that flatterers refuse to see
faults even when they are as huge as Olympus. Fail-
ing to get the declaration concerning their friendship
that he expected, Cassius does a little piece of emotional acting. He addresses Antony and young Octavius, begging them to come and revenge themselves
on Cassius alone, for Cassius is a-weary of the world;
hated by one he loves; defied by his brother; re-
buked like a slave; all his faults observed, set down
in a notebook, studied and recited by heart to be
cast into his teeth. He has changed to the first person at the end of the long sentence. O, he could
weep his very spirit from his eyes in the form of tears,
he exclaims. He offers his dagger to Brutus and bares
his breast, telling him that within that breast will be
found a heart more precious than Pluto's [3] mine and
richer than gold. If Brutus be a Roman, he may take
this heart. This does not seem to be an offer to his
country, but to Brutus personally, since all the re-
mainder of the address is to the individual. This is
borne out in the next sentence where he offers Brutus

[3] Some editions have "Plutus' " and some "Pluto's". Both were
gods of riches.

his heart after denying, or seeming to deny him, gold. He bids Brutus strike as he did at Cæsar, declaring that he knows that when he hated Cæsar most he loved him better than he ever loved Cassius. The Arden editors find that Cassius has made a "desperate effort to govern his temper, not from fear, for he never shows any sign of cowardice, but because of his personal affection for Brutus." They find in this scene "another example of the extent to which Cassius is swayed by purely personal feeling, as shown in the whole tone of his attack on Cæsar."

Brutus is deeply moved, and says in a husky voice, "Sheathe your dagger." Cassius may be angry when he will, he grants, and his anger may have free play. Cassius may do as he pleases and even a dishonorable action will be regarded as belonging to the mood of the moment. He assures Cassius that he is associated with a lamb-like person (himself) in whom anger lies sleeping as fire lies dormant in a flint, a quiet person who, when treated with force, may show a hasty spark and immediately be calm again. Cassius has been deeply hurt by one of Brutus' speeches and asks now if he has lived to be but mirth and laughter to his friend Brutus at times when he is troubled by grief and dominated by ill-temper. Brutus admits that, when he spoke as he did, he was ill-tempered too. Cassius is happy to have him confess as much and offers his hand. Brutus offers his heart, too. Cassius begins to speak, but gets no further than "O, Brutus!" Brutus inquires sympathetically what it is he is struggling with, and Cassius asks if Brutus has not love enough for him to bear with him when that proneness to passionate outbreaks ("rash humour"), which he inherits from his mother, makes him forgetful of his love for his friend. Brutus says quietly that he does have that much love for Cassius and that henceforth whenever Cassius is too severe ("over-earnest") with him, he will think it is his mother who chides and leave him alone. Does it seem that Cassius is taking more than his share of the blame here and permitting Brutus to be magnanimous? There are wide differences of opinion as to which was the aggressor in this scene. The student must not permit his admiration for one personality to blind him to Shakespeare's character delineation. Brutus has, up to this time, been the more noble of the two, but we cannot insist on reading nobility where Shakespeare has traced its falling off. Brutus has so captured the fancy of many scholars that they cannot conceive of his being more to blame than Cassius for anything. Shakespeare's characters are not cast in a mould. They grow stronger and finer or deteriorate—or there would be no object in reading the plays. Even the stoutest admirer of Brutus must be prepared to find his integrity suffering under the experiences that have come to him—if such deterioration is found in the lines of the play. The student should be on the alert, too, to discover whether Brutus has lost sight of the high ideal he once held for the future of Rome. It is a great tragedy to lose a high ideal, a deeper tragedy, sometimes, than losing one's life and one's opportunity, as was the case with Cæsar. This discovery of retrogression, if it should be made, need not seriously hinder the student's agreement with MacCallum when he says that after "the appalling discovery that his party is animated by selfish greed and not by righteousness, and that Cæsar bore away the palm in character as well as ability", Brutus still bears up under "the sustaining consciousness that he himself acted for the best, and the pathetic imagination even now that the rest must live up to his standard."

The generals' quarrel has been heard by those outside and they are interrupted by the entrance of a poet. The intrusion "rouses Brutus to indignation; but the presumptuous absurdity of it tickles Cassius' sardonic humor." [4] The episode is the dramatization of an incident recorded by Plutarch. As Douglas Bush puts it "Shakespeare's method was to soak himself in Plutarch and then use his imagination."

Brutus takes command of the military needs of the moment and orders the men on guard at the door to instruct the commanders to lodge their companies for the night. Cassius asks the two to return as soon as this is done and bring Messala with them. The two go out and Brutus orders Lucius to bring a bowl of wine. Cassius sits down at a table (at least we may think of him as standing up to this time) and says he would not have believed that Brutus could be

[4] MacCallum.

so angry. Brutus breaks out with the statement that he is full of many griefs, and Cassius refers him to his philosophy for help. His Stoicism should teach him that nothing evil can come to him. Brutus assures Cassius that no man bears sorrow better than he—but Portia is dead. Cassius can understand a personal sorrow, for personal relationships are strong with him; and, after an incredulous exclamation, he asks how he escaped killing when he crossed Brutus as he has done. He exclaims on the insupportable and touching loss and then asks what sickness caused Portia's death. Brutus relates how, longing for her husband's return and being grieved that Octavius and Antony were gathering an army to go against her husband's party, she swallowed fire during the absence of her servants. The story of Portia's swallowing fire is told by Plutarch. Modern scholars consider it improbable that she used such means.

Lucius enters with the wine and Brutus takes it from his hands, saying he is eager to bury all unkindness. Have they really come to any satisfactory and reasonable agreement about the accusations that have been made? Cassius says his very heart is thirsty to drink Brutus' noble pledge. He asks Lucius to fill the cup to overflowing, adding that he cannot drink too much of Brutus' love. Titinius is at the door and comes in with Messala. There is no mention in the Folio or in modern editions that Lucilius returns with them. Brutus welcomes the newcomers, inviting them to sit about the taper, and says they will consider the necessary war preparations. But Cassius is still thinking of Portia. Cassius has married Brutus' sister and we may well believe that the four of them had spent many pleasant hours together. Cassius feels Portia's death keenly. Unlike Cæsar, he was more strongly moved by his emotions than by his reason. In this place it makes him quite lovable, does it not? Brutus begs him to speak no more of Portia and turns to Messala and asks of letters he has had from Rome. The news is, he tells Messala, that Octavius and Antony are coming upon them with a mighty army, moving toward Philippi. Messala, too, has had that report and Brutus asks what additional news his letters have brought. Messala tells of the death of a hundred senators who have fallen under the proscription of the triumvirs. Brutus has had this news, too, but his information gave the number of senators as seventy. Among the number was Cicero. Cassius arouses himself at the news of Cicero's death. Messala asks if Brutus has had letters from his wife, and Brutus denies that he has. Messala tells the story that Brutus has just told to Cassius. Whether we find evidence here of revision of the play, as some scholars think, or whether Brutus permits Messala to tell the story to save himself the pain of explanation, or whether, sitting in a council of war, he thinks it his duty to put aside personal grief, we do not know. Other suggestions have been made—one that Brutus may make these inquiries with the hope that Messala's letter will contradict the one he has received. Mark Van Doren suggests that this may be a piece of acting on the part of Brutus. He says in part: "Neither would he admit that his behavior to Messala when Messala brings him the news of Portia's death is a piece of acting. . . . He would call it a demonstration of how Stoic gentlemen should conduct themselves. And in truth it is. Brutus already knows of Portia's death, for we have heard him telling Cassius of it. Cassius then is assisting him in the act, and Messala is being impressed as he should be. It is not vanity. It is virtue, it is true manhood demonstrating itself for the benefit of others. But to say as much is again to say that Brutus is humorlessly good. If his duty is to know himself, his performance fails. Nobility has numbed him until he cannot see himself for his principles. . . . His conquest of himself has extended to his wit; his excellence is not inconsistent with a certain lethargy of mind." What Brutus says to Messala is that we must all die and in thinking that Portia can die but once he can find fortitude to bear it. Messala says it is thus that great men should bear their losses, and Cassius adds that he has as strong principles, or fortitude ("art") as Brutus, yet his nature could not bear such grief so well. MacCallum comments, "It is not his philosophy but his character that gives him strength to bear the grief of Portia's death."

Well, they are still alive, seems to be Brutus' next thought, and they must get to work. Or, as has been

suggested, he may mean, our work is alive and therefore requires attention more than the dead. He asks
Cassius' opinion of marching to Philippi immediately. Cassius does not think well of the plan and
Brutus asks his reason. Cassius gives it: It is better
that the enemy seek them, for in doing so they will
waste their supplies, weary their soldiers, and do
themselves injury, while we, remaining where we
are, will be rested and be nimbly on the defense.
These are good reasons, Brutus agrees, but he has
even better ones, and he names them. The people
between Philippi and Sardis are of questionable loyalty to them (the Brutus-Cassius forces) because they
have had to contribute to their campaign fund,
which they have done reluctantly. The enemy,
marching through their territory, will add many of
these rebellious people to their number and will come
on refreshed and encouraged by the addition of these
recruits. By going on to Philippi, they will cut off
the enemy from these additional numbers and leave
the local discontent behind them. Cassius has a further word, or an objection, but is not permitted to
speak and Brutus goes on after begging Cassius'
pardon for the interruption. Cassius must remember
other advantages besides those just mentioned. He
names them: They have tried the friends about them
to the limit; their legions are brim-full; their cause
is ripe. But the enemy is increasing every day while
they have reached their limit and will soon be on
the decline. He then speaks the now familiar lines,

"There is a tide in the affairs of men,
Which, taken at the flood, leads on to fortune;
Omitted, all the voyage of their life
Is bound in shallows and in miseries."

They are now floating on this crucial tide, Brutus concludes, and they must take the current when it serves their purpose or lose their venture. When the seasoned Shakespearean student comes to such passages as this in successive readings of the play he finds his thought turning to Hudson's exclamation, "The idea of a book-worm riding the whirlwind of war!" Beautiful as Brutus' present thought it, does it constitute an adequate, practical theory to set against the trained military experience of an old campaigner like Cassius? Is there anything very definite about legions being "brim-full," their cause being "ripe" and their enemy "increasing"? Does not military strategy need to deal with exact numbers and definitely known conditions? Cassius yields to Brutus as he has done before and agrees that, according to Brutus' wish, they will march forward and meet the enemy at Philippi. The distance between Sardis and Philippi was more than a hundred miles as the crow flies, but Shakespeare makes it a short distance.

Brutus calls attention to the lateness of the hour, adding that human nature must obey the necessary demands for sleep, and they must now pay this demand, though somewhat niggardly, with a little rest. He asks if there is anything further to discuss. Cassius says there is nothing more and bids Brutus good-night with the suggestion that they rise early to be on their way. Brutus calls Lucius to bring his gown (rather a strange action to us, since he was the host of the occasion) and continues to bid the others good-night. When he comes to Cassius, he says earnestly, "Noble, noble Cassius, good-night and good repose." Professor Kittredge finds that this speech "from the habitually self-controlled Brutus is enough to show that he does not believe his 'brother' guilty of 'selling and marting his offices for gold'." Cassius is still full of regrets over the quarrel and expresses the hope that such a rift may never come between them again. Brutus assures him that everything is "well" between them. Cassius gives him a seemingly more formal good-night, which, no doubt, is intended to show a certain deference, addressing him as "my lord". Brutus bids him good-night as a brother. Titinius and Messala bid good-night to "Lord Brutus" and Brutus embraces all of them in a final farewell. Shakespeare's parting scenes are always delightful in their charming graciousness.

Lucius enters with his master's gown and Brutus asks about his instrument, then, noticing the boy's drowsy tones, says he does not blame him for being tired because he has spent more time than usual in watching. He bids him call the military guards and announces his intention of having them sleep on cushions in his tent. The men are called and Brutus makes the proposal, giving as his reason the possi-

bility of having to call them to go on business to
Cassius. The men assure him of their willingness
to stand guard in the usual way as long as he wishes,
but Brutus says he will not have it so. He makes the
excuse that there may be other reasons than the one
he has named that may require their near presence.
Brutus is always kind and considerate of dependents.
The men prepare to lie down and Brutus, running
his hand into the pocket of the dressing-gown, finds
the "book" he was looking for. Could the books of
the Roman world be easily carried in a man's
pocket? How about the books of Shakespeare's
time? What was the size of many of them? Lucius was sure, he says, that his master had not given
the book to him. Brutus' next line suggests that he
may have placed some blame on the boy for the lost
book, but he apologizes, begging him to have patience
with his forgetfulness. Then he asks if Lucius can
stay awake long enough to play a strain or two, and
Lucius consents. Brutus fears he troubles the boy
too much, but Lucius says it is his duty. Brutus
would not urge his duty beyond his strength, he
assures the boy, because he knows young people need
their rest. Lucius says he has already slept a little
and Brutus promises not to keep him long. Then he
adds the sad note that if he lives—beyond the coming battle—he will be good to the boy. Lucius begins to play and sing sleepily and Brutus addresses
Murderous Sleep to ask if he has placed an arresting,
heavy staff (as a sheriff's officer might do) upon the

boy who plays for him. He speaks to the "knave" (boy servant) and bids him good-night. He will not do him so much wrong as to wake him, he says sympathetically. He notices the boy's position and sees that a slight move may break the instrument, and he takes it away gently. Then he sits down and turns to his book, trying to locate the place where he left off reading. He has found it and remarks that the taper is burning badly.[5]

To continue the story with Quiller-Couch, "Was the taper burning ill or was there a shadow deepening beyond it? He looked up. It was a shadow, but it had shape-likeness; it was dead Cæsar standing there! Brutus' blood ran cold as he stared at the apparition. It seemed to him that he found voice to challenge it. 'Speak—what art thou?'

> 'Thy evil spirit, Brutus!'
> 'Why comest thou?'
> 'To warn thee thou shalt see me at Philippi!'

Between the dread and scorn of himself and incredulity Brutus echoed the words stupidly, almost with a laugh.

> ' "At Philippi" the vision repeated.
> Why I will see thee then at Philippi.'

Brutus brought his fist down on the table calling, 'Lucius Varro! Claudius! Awake there!' and looked

---

[5] There was a tradition in Shakespeare's time that candles fluttered at the approach of a supernatural object.

again. The vision had vanished.[6] 'The strings are out of tune, my lord,' muttered the boy Lucius drowsily.

"Brutus awoke him: awoke the soldiers. Why had they cried in their sleep? What had they seen? They had seen nothing. Had they cried out? It was strange but indeed they had seen nothing.

"Had Brutus, too, seen nothing? Perhaps. But the spirit of Cæsar—all that Cæsar had stood for, all that he had meant upon earth—awaited them on the plains of Philippi, toward which Brutus and Cassius set forth next day."

A question presents itself here: Did William Shakespeare believe in ghosts? We may reasonably believe that he was well in advance of his age in his attitude toward superstition, but we have no definite knowledge of his personal belief in the supernatural. Witches, ghosts, and apparitions offered effective dramatic material for the playwright's use. They could be made objective or subjective. But always in the hands of Shakespeare, they were connected with the conscience of man and the working out of destiny; and we may be certain that, while William Shakespeare, the dramatist, was working for striking theatrical effects, William Shakespeare, the psychologist, was searching deep and long into the souls of

[6] Referring to the text, it will be found that Brutus did not call until the Ghost was gone—but the discovery need not interfere with this dramatic version of the story, except to raise the question whether Brutus was courageous enough to strike his fist on the table in the presence of the Ghost.

men. Consequently, lovers of Shakespeare may be very glad that the people of Elizabethan England believed in ghosts.

MacCallum comments as follows on the ghostly visitation: "The regrets and forebodings of Brutus appear before him in outward form. All day the mischievousness of his intervention has been present to his mind; now his accusing thoughts take shape in the vision of the murdered friend, and his vague presentiment of retribution at Philippi leap to consciousness in its prophetic words. But all of this does not abash his soul or shake his purpose. He only hastens the morning march.

"Thus he moves to his doom, and never was he so great. He is stripped of all adventitious aids. His private affections are wrecked, and the thought of his wife has become a torture. Facts have given the lie to his belief that his country has chosen him as her champion. He can no longer cherish the thought that his course has been a benefit to the Roman world."

Sir John Squire finds that the closing lines of this scene describe the hush before catastrophe—"a time in which we may expect to find the strain of the soul near the breaking point." This author continues, speaking of Shakespeare's descriptions of nights that precede crime or irrevocable doom, "In *Julius Cæsar* there are two such; the night before Philippi is the consequence and the parallel of the night before the murder of Cæsar. In both is a great event prepared by whispers amid darkness that awaits the inevitable and relentless dawn, which brings once the deliberate slaying and once its retribution. Brutus and the boy are in both. But at Philippi the boy, symbolically, has grown tired, and Brutus, still resolute in his narrow nobility, is as one who has grown too tired to sleep, and has nothing left in life but to await the last fight and die well. He has shed his autumnal foliage and his tree stands with bare and writhen limbs against the stars . . . in the tragedies [there is] an atmosphere, a situation which must of its own nature break, a mighty arching wave, curved to its thinnest crest and an instant at rest before it topples in reverberating ruin. The hand of Shakespeare was, when he willed, unerring in preparation for catastrophe, and his finest endings are unparalleled in literature."

ACT V—SCENE I

BRUTUS had overruled Cassius in the matter of moving on to Philippi (making use of the advantage he had gained in the quarrel scene, in the opinion of MacCallum), and they are now approaching their destination. We find Octavius and Antony in camp awaiting their arrival. Antony has said they would not come down, probably having in mind that that would be the military decision of Cassius. He does not know how much of leadership has been taken over by Brutus.

Octavius informs Antony of the coming of the enemy and adds that Brutus and Cassius mean to summon ("warn") them to battle here at Philippi before they (Octavius and Antony) have had time to present their claims. Antony says he understands their inner thoughts and knows why they do this. They could be content, or might prefer, he thinks, to come upon ("visit") them at other places, yet they descend with a terrible show of bravery, thinking by this bold front to give the impression of courage. Yet, it is not true that they are brave, Antony adds.

A messenger enters with the news that the enemy is coming on with a great show of gallantry. Their red flag, signifying the intention of an immediate attack, is displayed and something is about to be done immediately.

Antony instructs Octavius to take command of the left side of the level plain, but Octavius asserts himself and says very decidedly that he will take the right hand and Antony is to take the left. Antony asks why the younger man crosses him in this emergency ("exigent") and Octavius disclaims crossing Antony, but again declares his intention of taking the right hand, admitting no question of his prerogative. However, the editors of the *Tudor Shakespeare* say, "Octavius yields for the moment, but threatens future opposition." They march toward the approaching army as if for a parley.

The "tyrannicides", as they now call themselves, enter, and Brutus notices that the opposing army has stopped as if wishing to speak to them. Cassius orders Titinius to stand with the troops while he and Brutus go forward.

Octavius asks his companion in arms if they shall give the signal for battle, and Antony answers, "No, Cæsar," adding that they will meet the others' charge when it comes. The generals, Brutus and Cassius, wish to have some words, he has noticed. Octavius orders their men not to stir until a signal is given.

Brutus advances and, addressing their opponents as "my countrymen," suggests that they make use of words before resorting to blows. Octavius makes the sharp reply that they do not love words better than blows, as Brutus does. Brutus offers the opinion that good words are better than bad strokes, and Antony comes in with a direct reference to the assassination, reminding Brutus that with his "bad," or wicked, strokes he can give good words, as when he made a hole in Cæsar's heart and cried, "Long live! hail, Cæsar!" Cassius addresses himself to Antony and says it is not known where he will succeed in planting his blows, but for his words they are sweeter than the honey of the bees of Hybla, in Sicily. The reference seems to be to his ingratiating words to the assassins after the death of Cæsar. Antony tauntingly suggests that his words are not stingless, too. Brutus answers that the words are both stingless and soundless, because Antony has stolen the bees' habit of humming and, very wisely, threats before he stings. Antony puts aside all quibbling and speaks with brutal frankness. He calls them villains and says they gave no warning when their vile daggers hacked one another in the sides of Cæsar; for then they showed their teeth with the treachery of smiling apes, fawning like hounds and bowing like bondmen, even kissing Cæsar's feet while Casca, like the cur he is, struck Cæsar on the neck. Sneeringly he ends, "O you flatterers!" Cassius resents the accusation of "flattery" and turns to Brutus, reminding him that he may thank himself for the insult. Antony's tongue would not have offended so to-day, he declares, if Cassius might have had his way in killing Antony with Cæsar.

Octavius calls on them to stop their bickering and

come to the business in hand, which is the cause. If arguing makes them overheated, he goes on, the endeavor to make good their arguments ("proof of it") will produce redder drops, or blood, in place of perspiration. He draws his sword [1] and holds it aloft, saying it is drawn against conspirators. He asks when they think the sword will be sheathed again, and answers the question himself. That will never come to pass, he declares, until Cæsar's three and thirty wounds be well avenged or till another Cæsar (meaning himself) has, by his death at their hands, added further slaughter to the traitors' swords. Brutus, addressing him as "Cæsar," assures him that he cannot die by traitors' hands unless they be found among his own following. Octavius hopes this is true and expresses his conviction that he was not born to be killed by Brutus. Brutus assures him (loftily?) that he could not die more nobly, even if he were the noblest of his strain—the Julii. But Cassius gibes back that Octavius is only a peevish schoolboy undeserving of death by Brutus' sword, adding as a thrust at Antony that this schoolboy is joined with a masker and a reveler. Antony replies with a not-too-pleasant laugh, or perhaps a sneer, It's the same old Cassius! Octavius urges Antony to come away and give up the conference which is getting nowhere. To the "traitors" he says they now hurl defiance in their teeth, challenging them to come to the field when

---

[1] Some editors have "a sword", some "this sword". There is a slight difference in meaning.

they dare, or when they have the stomach for fighting. Octavius and Antony go out.

Cassius knows the storm is at hand and bids the winds blow and the billows to swell. Their bark must swim the storm now, he says, and all they have is at hazard. Brutus calls to Lucilius and they speak aside. There is no apparent reason for this action except the opportunity it affords Cassius of speaking to Messala about things he might not be willing to confide to Brutus. Cassius turns to Messala and speaks to him at length, partly in reminiscent vein. To-day is his birthday, he begins. He asks Messala to take his hand and witness that, against his will, as Pompey had done, he is compelled to risk all their liberties on one battle. He speaks of his philosophy and confesses that he has changed his mind about the teachings of Epicurus (that the gods do not trouble themselves about human affairs) and has come to believe in omens (which, in Greek and Roman thought, were phenomena or circumstances foreboding good or evil).[2] He tells of an experience he has had coming from Sardis. Two mighty eagles swooped down upon their foremost ("former") ensign, and perched there, gorging and feeding from the soldiers' hands. They followed the army to Philippi, but have disappeared this morning. And in their place ravens, crows, and kites fly over the heads of the soldiers, looking down at them as if

---

[2] "Omens were seen notably in the flight of and song of birds, and in lightning and thunder, according to the direction in which these were seen or heard."—*Oxford Companion to Classical Literature*.

they were already sickly prey. Their shadows form a dark, fatal canopy over the army, which seems ready to give up the ghost. Messala begs him not to put faith in such things, and Cassius says he believes them only partly, then rallies himself and adds that, in spite of these forebodings, his spirits are fresh and he is resolved to meet all perils resolutely.

Brutus closes his conversation with Lucilius and joins the others. Cassius speaks to him, addressing him as "most noble Brutus" and expressing the hope that the gods may stand friendly to-day in order that they who are friends of peace may live out their days to old age. But, he continues, since the affairs of men always remain uncertain, it is best that they reckon with the worst that may befall. A sadder note comes into his voice as he goes on to say that, if they lose this battle, then this is the last time they will ever speak together. What, in this event, is Brutus prepared to do, he asks. Brutus answers that, according to his Stoic philosophy which made him blame Cato for taking his own life, he will arm himself with patience and await ("stay") the providential decree of such high powers as govern the world. Parenthetically, he has said he does not know why, but he finds it cowardly to commit suicide because of what might befall. Then, Cassius asks, if the battle is lost, is Brutus satisfied to be led in triumph through the streets of Rome? And Brutus answers with a decided and impressive, "No!" Brutus will never go bound to Rome, he declares. Perhaps he had not thought of this possibility until Cassius mentioned it. No, Brutus bears too great a mind, he says. But this day, he goes on, must finish what the Ides of March began. And now he, too, reflects that this may be their last farewell. Again they are two very close friends facing possible death on the battlefield. Whether they shall ever meet again he does not know, Brutus continues, therefore it is fitting that they take their everlasting farewell. Then he says,

> "For ever, and for ever farewell, Cassius!
> If we do meet again, why, we shall smile;
> If not, why then, this parting was well made."

And Cassius replies,

> "For ever, and for ever, farewell, Brutus!
> If we do meet again, we'll smile indeed;
> If not, 'tis true this parting was well made."

Perhaps this is the noblest parting scene in all Shakespeare. If the student, in reading it, cannot hear the catch in Brutus' voice when he says, "If not, why then" and sense the lump in the throat of Cassius when, too overcome to find words of his own, he repeats almost verbatim the words of Brutus, he has yet to learn how to read Shakespeare, and has missed much of Shakespeare's delineation of a beautiful friendship.

It is Brutus who breaks the spell of this august moment by giving command to lead on, but he immediately expresses the wish that they might know the outcome of the day's business. Then with resignation he adds that it is sufficient that the day will end and that the end will be known. MacCallum says of this speech, "Suspense is intolerable to his sensitive and eager soul. Ere the battle begins he can hardly bear the uncertainty."

Have not both of these men, in this hour of need, thrown their philosophy to the winds? Why? In the spiritual life no philosophy can take the place of personal experience. One wonders if Shakespeare has not been suggesting here and there throughout the play that Cæsar's life was rich in spiritual experience, while the lives of Brutus and Cassius, with all their philosophy, were poor. There is another Shakespearean character, a rarely beautiful soul, who was at bay in an evil world, in a kind of forest of primitive sin, with only his own keen mind as a defensive weapon, who might have said to them, There are more things in heaven and earth, my Roman friends, than are dreamt of in your philosophy!

ACT V—SCENE II

WE FIND Brutus and Messala on the battlefield.
Brutus gives Messala written instructions, or "bills",
to carry to their legions on the other side of the field.
He says he notices indifferent fighting in the wing
commanded by Octavius, and is of the opinion that
a sudden push will overthrow them. With seeming
enthusiasm he bids Messala ride and let "them",
probably his forces, all come down.

ACT V—SCENE III

In ANOTHER part of the field, Cassius is distraught.
He is telling Titinius how their own soldiers have
fled from the enemy and how he has turned enemy
to his own men. He points to an ensign and says it
was turning back, but he (Cassius) slew the man who
carried it and took the flag from him. Titinius says
Brutus gave the word too early, because, having
some advantage over Octavius, he took it too eagerly.
His soldiers fell to taking spoils and the army of
Cassius was surrounded by Antony. Pindarus enters
and excitedly urges Cassius to fly, telling him that
Antony has taken possession of his tents. Cassius
ascends a little hill and says this is far enough for
him to fly. He asks Titinius to look and see if his
tents are on fire. Titinius replies that they are. Cassius directs Titinius to mount his (Cassius') horse
and ride hard and fast to "yonder troops" and return
quickly to let him know whether the troops are
friends or enemies. Titinius responds readily and
goes. Cassius then asks Pindarus to go to a higher hill
and watch the progress of Titinius and report what
he may see about the field. Cassius' distant sight is
not good enough for him to do this himself. Pindarus
goes and, when he is left alone, we find how Cassius'

courage is ebbing. He begins to think he is destined to die on his birthday, that his life has run its compass, its full circle. Pindarus calls from above and tells him that Titinius is being surrounded by horsemen. In broken lines, because of his excitement, he describes the scene as it appears to him and reports that horsemen ride toward him using their spurs; yet Titinius spurs on; now they almost overtake him; now some alight and Titinius alights too. They shout for joy and Pindarus concludes that Titinius is captured. Cassius tells him to come down and behold no more. He chides himself as a coward to have lived so long as to see his best friend (Titinius) taken before his face. It will be noticed that he places Titinius above Brutus in his affection.

Pindarus comes down and Cassius reminds him of the time when he took him prisoner in Parthia, thus saving his life. Cassius had made him swear always to do his bidding. Now, he says, he is going to ask Pindarus to keep his oath and it will make him a freeman. Pindarus must take Cassius' sword, the one that he ran through Cæsar's bowels, and run it through his master's body. Cassius will tolerate no argument about it, he says. He extends the sword with its handle toward Pindarus and tells him to guide it when he has covered his face. Pindarus keeps his oath. As Cassius dies, he thinks of Cæsar and addresses him, saying that he is revenged with the same sword that killed him. Pindarus is now free, but regrets the deed he has been compelled to commit. He is glad to escape from Roman captivity, however, and leaves the scene quickly.

Titinius and Messala enter and we hear the result of the battle. Brutus has overthrown Octavius and Antony has overthrown the legions of Cassius. Titinius is hoping that the tidings will bring some comfort to Cassius. The two men look anxiously for Cassius. Titinius says he left him with Pindarus, all disconsolate. They discover the body and to Titinius the setting sun of Cassius means that the sun of Rome has set, and her day is gone. Clouds, dews, and damp dangers may come, for their deeds are done. It was because he feared for my success that he has done this deed, Titinius concludes. Titinius thus takes to himself the blame for Cassius' death, but Messala says it was mistrust of the general success of the battle. He then addresses hateful Error, who, he says, is the child of Melancholy, and asks why she shows things that are not true to the intelligent thoughts of men. Error, he adds, that is so soon born out of Melancholy, kills its mother as vipers are supposed to do. The meaning seems to be that Error has killed the person who became melancholy, namely Cassius. Titinius has begun looking for Pindarus and Messala says he will go to meet Brutus while Titinius seeks further. When he meets Brutus he will "thrust" the report of Cassius' death in his ears. Then, he adds, his word "thrust" well expresses his meaning because the news will be as welcome to Brutus as piercing steel and envenomed darts.

Titinius encourages Messala to look for Brutus. When left alone he addresses the prostrate form of Cassius, asking why he sent him forth. In further moving questions to the dead man the error is revealed. Pindarus had given the wrong report. Instead of being surrounded by enemies, Titinius had been welcomed by the friends of Cassius. They had put a victor's garland on his brow, and Brutus had sent a garland to Cassius. Alas, Titinius exclaims, Cassius has misconstrued everything! He stoops and places on the dead man's brow the garland that Brutus has sent, saying,

> "Thy Brutus bid me give it thee, and I
> Will do his bidding."

He addresses Brutus, asking him to come quickly and see how much he, Titinius, loved Caius Cassius. He begs leave of the gods, saying this is the Roman way to die, and kills himself with Cassius' sword. This is the finest possible commentary on Cassius—that he had a friend who would die for him.

Brutus enters with Messala and others. They have come to find the body of Cassius, and discover the dead Titinius also. Brutus recognizes the might of Julius Cæsar at work and says his spirit is walking abroad and turning their swords into their own [1] entrails. It is this "spirit" that has dominated the play—a great spiritual force that outlived the frail

---

[1] The word "proper" merely strengthens the word "own"—*New Clarendon Shakespeare.*

body. It was this "spirit" that Brutus had wished to destroy without killing the body, having no comprehension of its meaning and confusing it with ambition. Professor Kittredge says, "The significance of the speech in determining the central motive of the play has been recognized by the best critics. The last two acts are bound to the first three by this conception."

Cato exclaims over the brave Titinius and calls attention to the garland he has placed on Cassius' head. Brutus asks if there still live any such Romans as these two. He bids farewell to the dead men, calling them the "last of all the Romans," adding that it is impossible that Rome shall ever again breed one of their kind. To the friends about him he says he owes more tears to Cassius than they will see him pay. To Cassius he promises that he will find time to sorrow for him. Gervinus says, "He puts off the debt of tears, that his personal anguish may not endanger the public cause." MacCallum says, "Flushed with his initial success, he expects to triumph and to live, and the years to come seem darkened with grief for his 'brother'."

Brutus orders the body of Cassius sent to Thasos, an island off the coast of Thrace, not far from Philippi. He says there will be no funeral in the camp lest it dishearten them. He calls to the individual officers about him, reminding them that it is three o'clock and that they must try their fortunes a second time before nightfall.

ACT V—SCENE IV

AGAIN they are on the battlefield and Brutus and his cousin, young Cato, are rallying their men. Brutus begs them to hold up their heads. Young Cato says he will go about the field and proclaim his name to the men, meaning to encourage them by memories of his father's military deeds and his record of patriotism. Perhaps Brutus has made his exit before Cato finishes the speech. The *First Folio* has the stage direction "Enter soldiers and fight". Not all modern editions keep this direction. The *Folio* does not credit the lines that follow to anyone, thus making them a continuation of Cato's speech. Most modern editors credit them to Brutus and miss the meaning of the passage. Following the *Folio,* it seems reasonable to credit the lines to Cato, and so we should find him suddenly posing as Brutus to deceive the enemy. Cato is slain. The *First Folio* does not have the stage direction "Exit" after the speech ending "know me for Brutus." Lucilius pauses for a moment to pay a tribute to Cato, saying he died as bravely as Titinius and may now be honored as Cato's son. A soldier enters and demands that Lucilius yield and Lucilius offers first to bribe him, but, using the ruse of Cato, he, too, poses as Brutus and tells his captor to kill him and claim the honor. The soldier and his companions accept his word and believe that they have captured Brutus. They decide to send word to Antony that Brutus is taken.

Antony enters and asks where the prisoner is. Lucilius speaks to Antony, knowing that he is recognized, and tells him that Brutus is safe. He assures him that no enemy will ever take alive the noble Brutus. He prays the gods to defend Brutus from so great a shame as being taken captive. He is certain that when Antony finds him he will be found like Brutus. Antony speaks to the soldier and tells him this man is not Brutus. Lucilius, however, is a worthy prize, too, and he orders the soldier to keep the captive safe, but to treat him with all kindness. Antony would rather have such men as Lucilius his friends than his enemies, he tells them. He orders some of the soldiers to go in search of Brutus and bring him word at Octavius' tent how everything has come out.

ACT V—SCENE V

BRUTUS and four others are removed from the fighting and Brutus suggests that they rest on a rock that is close by. The lines that follow need a little illumination from Plutarch. Stanilus had been sent to find out the condition of the army and was to hold up a torchlight if all was well. In order to do this he had to go through the ranks of the enemy. He held up the light, but did not return. Now they have concluded that he must have been slain. Brutus says slaying is the fashion. He whispers to Clitus and Clitus answers, "No, not for all the world!" Brutus bids him hold his peace and Clitus says he would rather kill himself; so we know what Brutus has requested of him. Brutus then whispers to Dardanius. Dardanius, too, refuses. Clitus and Dardanius discuss the matter between themselves, and notice that Brutus is meditating. Clitus pictures him as a noble vessel that is full—his grief overflowing from his eyes. Brutus calls Volumnius to him and tells him how Cæsar appeared to him two different times, at Sardis, and last night, here, at Philippi. He says he knows his hour is come. Volumnius says, "Not so, my lord", but Brutus is sure of it. Their enemies have beaten them to the verge of the grave, he goes on. Low alarums are heard, announcing the approach of the enemy. Brutus says it is more worthy for them to leap into the grave than to tarry until they are pushed in. He then appeals to the friendship of their school days and begs Volumnius to hold his sword while he runs on it, but Volumnius answers that such an act is not a service for a friend to render. The enemy is coming closer and Clitus urges Brutus to fly. Brutus bids farewell to them, including Strabo, who has been asleep. Addressing them as "country-men" he tells them that his heart rejoices that, in all his life, he has found no man that was not true to him. MacCallum says, "When none of his friends will consent to kill him, their very refusal, since it springs from love, fills his soul with triumph. It is characteristic that this satisfaction to his private affections ranks with him as supreme at the end of all." But is Brutus' statement true—the statement that, in all his life, no man had been untrue to him? The glory of having such friendships, the speaker goes on, is more to him than all that will come to Antony in his "vile conquest". Again he bids them farewell and says his tongue has almost ended his life's history. Eternal night is about to close his eyes, he is thinking; his body that has but labored toward this end would now go to its rest. Another alarum sounds and Brutus bids them fly, saying he will follow. Clitus, Dardanius, and Volumnius go, but Brutus detains Strabo. He reminds him that he is a man of good report, that his life has had some honor in it. Then he puts the question: will Strabo hold his sword while he runs on it? He repeats the question appealingly. Strabo requests that he give him his hand first in token of friendship and then he bids Brutus farewell. Brutus echoes the farewell and runs on the sword. Brutus' last words are:

> "Cæsar, now be still:
> I killed not thee with half so good a will."

MacCallum says of these lines, "He even seems at last to recognize his own guilt, for not only does he admit the might of Cæsar's spirit in the suicide of Cassius, but when his own turn comes, his dying words sound like a proffer of expiation."

Some thoughts from the following paragraph of Professor Lounsbury may be advantageously applied to the death of Brutus: "Pervading all these plays of Shakespeare which involve the problems that beset man's life and destiny is not the shallow conception of poetic justice . . . but instead the profound conviction he inspires of the sway and sweep of those moral forces which, once set in motion, must go on to work out their inevitable course in human conduct, whether it be itself right or wrong, whether it lead to triumph or to failure. . . . The idea that runs through it all, that unites its most discordant elements, that binds in one common bond its most diverse themes, is the existence of the reign of law; is the inexorable sequence of cause and effect, whether it bring with it joy or sorrow, whether it point to the serene close of happy days, or disclose itself in the ever-recurring tragedy of lives going out in defeat or countless quieter forms of failure. It is not at all that every act is followed by the specific result which is most appropriate to it, according to our imperfect conception of justice. It is that the general consequences of human conduct correspond in the Shakespearean drama with the consequences which we see exemplified in the life about us. In the domain of morals as in that of letters it is the art which holds the mirror up to nature."

Octavius and Antony enter, bringing Lucilius and Messala. Messala inquires about Brutus from Strabo, and is told that he is free from the bondage Messala is in. Then he adds, The conquerors can do no more to Brutus than to burn his body on the funeral pyre, for Brutus overcame himself and no one will have the honor of killing him. Lucilius is glad Brutus has taken this course. Octavius says he will take into his service all the men who followed Brutus. This was frequently done by conquerors. Octavius asks Strabo if he will serve him and Strabo answers that he will if Messala will recommend him. Messala asks about the manner of Brutus' death and Strabo tells how he ran on his sword. Messala then recommends Strabo to Octavius as the man who did the latest service to their master, Brutus. "By this touch we are assured of the essential nobility of Strabo's act in the opinion of his contemporaries." [1]

After Mark Antony's speech that now follows,

[1] Professor Kittredge.

Octavius gives orders that the body of Brutus shall lie in state in the speaker's own tent, and shall receive all honors due to his soldierly rank. Then he orders the sounding of the signal for the cessation of hostilities ("call the field to rest"). They will then away and share the glories of the happy day, he concludes.

But before Octavius had given these final instructions, Mark Antony had spoken the now familiar eulogy over the dead Brutus:

> "This was the noblest Roman of them all:
> All the conspirators save only he
> Did what they did in envy of great Cæsar;
> He only, in the general honest thought
> And common good to all, made one of them.
> His life was gentle, and the elements
> So mixed in him that Nature might stand up
> And say to all the world, 'This was a man!'"

It should be noted that Antony says that Brutus is the noblest of all the conspirators, not the noblest of all the Romans, as the popular conception has it. If he had ended here, it would not have been a great tribute to Brutus. But he goes on to explain that Brutus only joined the conspirators in an all-embracing, honest consideration for the common good.

And what are the "elements" that are so skillfully mixed in Brutus? Are they, as some have interpreted the line, the elements of Shakspeare's physical world, namely, earth, air, fire, and water? Surely not. Surely they must be the elements described by another Shakespearean character when he exclaimed,

"What a piece of work is man! how noble in reason! how infinite in faculty! in form and moving how express and admirable! in action how like an angel! in apprehension how like a god! the beauty of the world! the paragon of animals!"

But this man, this paragon of animals, has "seduced" his mind with its god-like reasoning power by consenting to the death of the noblest man who ever lived in the annals of time, not knowing that he was so situated that the "welfare of the State, and even, as it appears, that of the whole civilized world, depended upon the resolution at which he arrived." [2]

When we look back over the play, the figure of Julius Cæsar lying at the base of Pompey's statue sinks into insignificance as a scene of tragedy by comparison with that other scene where six men enter the garden of a friend at the dawn of a new day to take his hand in an inhuman, unholy pact.

And, reflecting further on these things, we may find ourselves saying with the poet,

> "Have I not reason to lament
> What man has made of man?"

[2] Brandes.